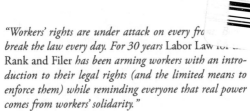

LABOR LAW FOR THE RANK & FILER
BUILDING SOLIDARITY WHILE STAYING CLEAR OF

By STAUGHTON LYND & DANIEL GROSS

"Workers' rights are under attack on every fr[o]
break the law every day. For 30 years Labor Law ₁₀₁ ₋₋
Rank and Filer *has been arming workers with an introduction to their legal rights (and the limited means to
enforce them) while reminding everyone that real power
comes from workers' solidarity."*
–**Alexis Buss**, former General Secretary-Treasurer,
  Industrial Workers of the World

"As valuable to working persons as any hammer, drill, sta-
pler, or copy machine, Labor Law for the Rank and Filer
is a damn fine tool empowering workers who struggle to
realize their basic dignity in the workplace while living
through an era of unchecked corporate greed. Smart,
tough, and optimistic, Staughton Lynd and Daniel Gross
provide nuts and bolts information to realize on-the-job
rights while showing us that another world is not only
possible but inevitable."
–**John Philo**, Legal Director, Maurice and Jane Sugar
  Law Center for Economic and Social Justice

"Some things are too important to leave to so called
'experts': our livelihoods, our dignity and our rights. In
this book, Staughton Lynd and Daniel Gross have provided us with a very necessary, empowering, and accessible
tool for protecting our own rights as workers."
–**Nicole Schulman**, co-editor, *Wobblies! A Graphic
  History* and *World War 3 Illustrated*

PM PRESS

LABOR LAW
FOR THE
RANK&FILER:
BUILDING SOLIDARITY
WHILE STAYING CLEAR OF THE LAW
SECOND EDITION

By STAUGHTON LYND&DANIEL GROSS

LABOR LAW FOR THE RANK&FILER:
BUILDING SOLIDARITY WHILE STAYING CLEAR OF THE LAW
By Staughton Lynd & Daniel Gross

Special thanks to Alice Lynd
Cover by Daniel Meltzer
Cover photo by Anna Karewicz

Published by:
PM Press, PO Box 23912, Oakland, CA 94623
www.pmpress.org

ISBN: 978-1-60486-419-9
Library Of Congress Control Number: 2010916478

10 9 8 7 6 5 4

Printed in the USA

CONTENTS

The Power of Secondary Pressure
Using Wage and Hour Claims
Saving Fringe Benefits
The Fight Against Shutdowns
No One Is Illegal
Cross-Border Solidarity

ACKNOWLEDGMENTS

The authors wish gratefully to acknowledge the assistance of Professors Jennifer Gordon of Fordham Law School and James Gray Pope of Rutgers Law School. Each carefully read a draft, and suggested additions and corrections.

We also appreciate the diligent research assistance of Sheila Maddali, Elizabeth McCurry, and Cristen Sargent.

Alice Lynd not only put the text in final form for publication but, along the way, made suggestions drawn from her own experience in employment law.

All remaining shortcomings having to do with strategic perspectives, tactical suggestions, citation to and characterization of precedents, or otherwise, are the responsibility of the authors.

CHAPTER I
ON BEING YOUR OWN LAWYER

MARTY AND STAN

This little book first appeared in 1978. A revised edition was published in 1982.

Two working-class intellectuals inspired the original booklet. The late Marty Glaberman spent years working for automobile companies in and around Detroit. He belonged to a radical group associated with the West Indian author and intellectual C.L.R. James. In 1952 Marty published a pamphlet entitled *Punching Out*.[1] There he argued that the characteristic achievement of the Congress of Industrial Organizations (CIO) was a collective bargaining agreement that contained a no-strike clause. Inevitably, Marty said, the union shop steward must enforce the contract, including its prohibition of work stoppages and wildcat strikes: the union steward becomes a cop for the boss.

During those same years, the late Stan Weir began his remarkable journey as a sailor, automobile worker, truck driver, and longshoreman. One of his basic ideas was that when human beings labor together they naturally create what Stan called informal work groups.[2] These associations

1   Martin Glaberman, *Punching Out & Other Writings*, ed. and introduced by Staughton Lynd (Chicago: Charles H. Kerr Publishing Company, 2002). See also Martin Glaberman, "Workers have to deal with their own reality and that transforms them," in *The New Rank and File*, ed. Staughton and Alice Lynd (Ithaca: Cornell University Press, 2000).

2   Stan Weir, *Singlejack Solidarity*, with a foreword by Norm Diamond and an afterword by George Lipsitz (Minneapolis: University of Minnesota Press, 2004). See also Stan Weir, "The Informal Work Group," in *Rank and File: Personal Histories by Working-Class*

arise in the workplace and cannot be transferred to a union hall away from the plant. The informal work group fosters workers' self-activity in the form of group grievances, wildcat work stoppages, and local general strikes.

Stan Weir also framed the question to which this booklet seeks to respond. When you go to work you ordinarily leave your constitutional rights as a citizen in the glove compartment of your car on the employer's parking lot. Is there anything in the law that can help us to enjoy as workers the rights to speak, to associate, and so on, that we have, at least on paper, away from work? Together with another longshoreman, Robert Miles, Stan formed a small publishing house, Singlejack Books, which printed the first two editions of *Labor Law for the Rank and Filer*.

The authors of this new edition generally endorse the ideas of our departed comrades, Marty Glaberman and Stan Weir. Daniel Gross is an organizer with the Industrial Workers of the World (IWW) on the campaign to organize Starbucks. A former Starbucks barista and a graduate of Fordham Law School, he is the Founding Director of Brandworkers International, a non-profit organization for retail and food employees. Staughton Lynd specialized in employment law as an attorney for Legal Services in Youngstown, Ohio, and has written, among other things, *Solidarity Unionism: Rebuilding the Labor Movement from Below* (Oakland: PM Press, 2015). Since his retirement in 1996 he has advocated for prisoners.

Organizers, ed. Alice and Staughton Lynd (New York: Monthly Review Press, 1988), and Stan Weir, "Unions with Leaders who Stay on the Job," in *We Are All Leaders: The Alternative Unionism of the Early 1930s*, ed. Staughton Lynd (Urbana: University of Illinois Press, 1996).

ON BEING YOUR OWN LAWYER

Basically, this is a do-it-yourself book. Its goal is to help you deal more effectively with the law: to protect yourself when the law is against you, and to get more accomplished when the law is on your side.

Our point of view is that whenever a problem can be solved without the help of a lawyer, do it. Besides being expensive the law takes a long time. And it is written and administered by individuals who for the most part do not understand or sympathize with the experience of working people.

Lawyers, like doctors, make their profession seem more mysterious than it really is. They use big words when short words would do just as well. They encourage workers to feel helpless unless a lawyer is representing them.

The assumption of this book is that, with a modest orientation, anyone able to read can make a **preliminary** assessment of a labor law problem. Dr. Spock takes the same approach to medicine in his famous book on baby care. He says to the mother or father of young children: if your child shows symptom A, watch carefully to see if B or C appear as well; if they do, call a doctor; if they don't, you can take care of the child yourself.

This book views your problems in labor law similarly. Our aim is not to teach you the law. It is to teach you how to teach yourself at least the broad outlines of the law, so that you can diagnose a labor law problem, just as you might size up what's wrong with the car engine.

To know what *the law* is about a problem, you have to know not only the text of the relevant statutes but also how that text has been interpreted by the National Labor Relations Board, by other administrative agencies, and by the courts.

If you work in a shop or office with a collective bargaining agreement and a grievance procedure, you have a head start in understanding this.

In using a grievance procedure, you have to know both the contract and decisions interpreting the contract. To rely on the text of the contract alone, no matter how clear it seems to be, can get you in **big** trouble.

Similarly, the law begins with the text of constitutions, statutes, administrative regulations, etc. But the law is more than these texts. It is also cases interpreting the texts.

THE BNA BOOKS

There is a set of books which can give you a general idea of what the law is about the most common labor law problems for workers employed by private companies. Some libraries have these books, some don't.

The Bureau of National Affairs (BNA) periodically publishes a book entitled *The Developing Labor Law*. It also publishes the *Labor Relations Expediter*.

It does not make sense to purchase the *Expediter* because it is in looseleaf form and is constantly updated by the BNA. If you can find a library that has this book it should be your first port of call when you want to look something up. It is arranged alphabetically; for instance, "Bargaining Units" comes before "Strikes." Use the index to try to determine what topic covers the problem you have in mind.

Every topic in the *Expediter* has a number, known as a "key number." The BNA periodically publishes a *Cumulative Digest* of cases. You can look in the *Digest* under the key number related to your problem and find short summaries of the important cases decided about that topic since the previous *Digest* was published.

Each case summary in the *Digest* has a citation to the full text of the decision. The decisions are collected in a series of volumes called the *Labor Relations Reference Manual*, or *LRRM* for short.

A citation lists in order: **the name of the case, the number of the volume in which the decision appears, the series of books of which that volume is a part, the page number on which the decision begins, and the date of the decision**. Thus, *Royal Typewriter Co.*, 85 LRRM 1501 (1974), tells you to get volume 85 of the *Labor Relations Reference Manual* and look on page 1501 for a 1974 decision involving the Royal Typewriter Company.

This is also the form used to cite court decisions: first the number of the volume, then the series, then the page of that volume on which the text of the decision begins, then the court, and finally the year. Thus, the case in which one of us sought to prevent U.S. Steel from closing its mills in Youngstown is *Local 1330 v. U.S. Steel*, 492 F.Supp. 1 (N.D. Ohio 1980). This translates as volume 492 of the series of volumes entitled Federal Supplement beginning on page 1 decided by the United States District Court for the Northern District of Ohio in 1980. The case then went to the circuit court of appeals. There it was decided with the citation *Local 1330 v. U.S. Steel*, 631 F.2d 1264 (6th Cir. 1980), "6th Cir." referring to the Sixth Circuit Court of Appeals for the states of Michigan, Ohio, Kentucky and Tennessee. The National Labor Relations Board has its own series of published decisions, using the abbreviation "NLRB." The NLRB citation may give you either the page number on which the decision begins or the number of the decision, as in *Sears, Roebuck & Co.*, 274 NLRB No. 55 (1985).

THE INTERNET

Internet-based resources are rapidly coming to dominate the legal research field and the labor law area is no exception. Lexis and Westlaw are the two leading fee based electronic research services but they can be costly for the rank and filer. Fortunately, the NLRB itself offers a multitude of free information on its website, www.nlrb.gov. Using a search engine, you can research the full text of documents including Administrative Law Judge decisions, Board decisions, and Advice Memos.

We cite cases, using the BNA system or the internet (or both), throughout this booklet. For the same reason, we have provided in footnotes the names of books or articles we think you might find helpful.

Of course, if possible you may wish a lawyer to double check your own research. (Often lawyers will provide a first consultation free of charge.) You should definitely consult a lawyer before finally deciding on a strategy involving the possibility of a lawsuit. And in a unionized workplace, it will make sense in most cases to consult with your union rep as well, **provided** you can do so without giving union officials the authority to veto the path you choose to solve the problem.

Often a strategy will involve a series of steps, each involving its own deadlines and procedural requirements. For example, a discharged worker might initially file for unemployment compensation; use the outcome to assess whether to file an employment discrimination claim or an NLRB charge within the six-month period applicable to each; and hold in reserve the possibility of a federal lawsuit.[3] You will be far more independent and self-sufficient

---

3 Another example of a strategy, which one of us is employing in the campaign to organize workers at Starbucks, is to make full use of the opportunity to file unfair labor practice charges with the National

if you have attempted to arrive at a first approximation of a strategy you want to use for yourself.

But one word of caution: The law changes. Before relying on any proposition or case citation in what follows, do your best to make sure that it is still—as lawyers say—"good law." You can determine whether a case is still good law by a process called "Shepardizing." To "Shepardize" is to determine in what later cases the precedent you have in mind has been cited. You can "Shepardize" a case at a law library or through one of the electronic research systems.

OF SWORDS AND SHIELDS

Think of law and lawyers as a last resort.

There is a widespread belief, especially when one is frustrated by grievance procedures, internal union appeals, or administrative complaints that seem to take forever, that it would go better before a judge. Don't believe it. The law takes at least as long. It is much more expensive. And lawyers will let you down as often as a grievance representative, if not more so.

The best way to think of the law is as a shield, not a sword. The law is not an especially good way to change things. But it can give you some real protection as you try to change things in other ways.

The law can also act as a net that restrains or co-opts efforts by workers to make change on the job. Therefore, an understanding of workplace law is a must for avoiding pitfalls to successful organizing.

Labor Relations Board while declining to become involved in asking the NLRB to conduct a union representation election. See Staughton Lynd and Daniel Gross, *Solidarity Unionism at Starbucks* (Oakland: PM Press, 2010).

CHAPTER 2
WHERE DO WORKERS' RIGHTS COME FROM?

The first answer many of us are likely to give to this question is: from the Constitution.

Every American likes to say to himself or herself, "I've got my rights." It's natural to suppose that our constitutional rights travel with us wherever we go.

But this answer is, unfortunately, wrong. The Constitution protects us only from action by the state, that is, the government. It does not protect us from **private** employers. If you work for a government, city, state or federal, you can claim constitutional rights to freedom of speech, to freedom from unreasonable search and seizure, to due process, to equality before the law. However, in the private sector the employer has no legal obligation to respect your constitutional rights.[4]

In the private sector, when you punch in you leave your constitutional rights behind. That's one of the reasons why it's so important for workers to take collective direct action without relying on the courts. In the private sector, you do not have a constitutional right to free speech: if your

---

4 The Thirteenth Amendment to the Constitution appears to be an exception to this generalization. Professor James Pope of Rutgers Law School points out that the Thirteenth Amendment prohibits slavery and involuntary servitude, without regard to who creates these conditions. See James Gray Pope, Peter Kellman and Ed Bruno, "Free Labor Today," *New Labor Forum* (Spring 2007), pp. 8–18; and James Gray Pope, "Labor's Constitution of Freedom," *Yale Law Journal*, v. 106 (1997), pp. 941–1031. Thus it might be possible to argue that when a private employer and a union negotiate a no-strike clause, they violate the Thirteenth Amendment even though there is no "state action."

employer makes an unsafe product, and you individually "blow the whistle" on him by informing the media, you may legally be fired for doing so. There is a dreadful line of cases in which employees have been held to be justly discharged because they made statements that were *disloyal* to the employer.

Likewise, in the private sector you are not innocent until proven guilty. Even within a unionized workplace, when an employer disciplines or discharges you, you don't stay on the job until the grievance is arbitrated. Instead, you are off work and lose pay, and get the money back only if you win the grievance.

Furthermore, most private sector employees are employed "at will," a pernicious doctrine adopted by judges during the unbridled capitalist expansion of the late nineteenth century. An "at will" employee can be fired, demoted, or receive a pay cut at any time for almost any reason, even a very bad reason, with no notice at all. This book will discuss those reasons for which an employer may **not** take adverse action against a worker, even an "at will" worker. We will also show that just because a boss may legally take an action does not preclude workers from contesting that action.

Thus, in the private sector the Constitution does not protect us, but there are two other sources that give us **some** of the same protections we enjoy, at least on paper, outside the workplace.

One source of rights in the private sector is the union and the collective bargaining agreement. At this writing, only 7.5% of private sector workers are in a unionized workplace. If you are one of them, it's a good idea to know the contract backward and forward, and to carry a copy on your person at all times.

Seniority, for instance, comes from the collective bargaining agreement. But seniority provides only partial equality before the law.[5] It ensures that the person who has worked longest will be laid off last, but it does not mean that foremen will be governed by the same rules as hourly employees. If an hourly worker starts a fight, he or she is likely to be fired because of a shop rule against fighting. But that rule doesn't necessarily apply to the foreman when **he** starts a fight. Thus the union and the collective bargaining agreement create a halfway citizenship, but not a full citizenship.

A second source of rights in the private sector is federal law. These rights were created by struggle. For instance, the struggle for the eight-hour day gained national prominence in 1886, when a sizable portion of the entire American labor movement took part in a political strike on its behalf. The international labor holiday, May Day, was one result. Time and a half pay for more than forty hours of labor in a week was finally recognized by Congress more than fifty years later in the Fair Labor Standards Act (the Wages and Hours Act) of 1938.

---

5 Indeed some have argued that seniority promotes **inequality**, especially in layoffs. Mia Giunta, an organizer for the United Electrical Workers (UE), describes a Connecticut plant she organized called F-Dyne Electronic. The workers were African American, African, Puerto Rican, Portuguese, Cuban and Mexican, and almost all women. She recalls: "Under the contract, the layoffs went according to seniority. We felt terrible, thinking of some of the workers who would be put out on the street.... [S]omebody suggested, 'We'll all work a few hours less each week. That way everybody can stay. Everybody will have health insurance.'... [A]nd that became the tradition in that factory." Mia Giunta, "Working-class people have a very deep culture based on solidarity and trust," in *The New Rank and File*, ed. Lynd and Lynd.

Similarly, in Illinois coal fields in the 1920s, local unions "adopted the rule that no man is going to work overtime without showing cause why no one else was available to share the work.... We got the company to go along by getting the key men in our union to cut down the production." Joe Ozanic, quoted in Carl Oblinger, *Divided Kingdom: Work, Community and the Mining Wars in the Central Illinois Coal Fields During the Great Depression* (Springfield: Illinois State Historical Society, 2004), p. 24.

A partial list of other rights recognized by federal law includes:

1. The right to engage in concerted activity for mutual aid and protection (Section 7 of the National Labor Relations Act).
2. The right not to be ordered by a federal court to stop such activity (Section 4 of the Norris-LaGuardia Act).
3. The right to refuse to perform abnormally dangerous work (Section 502 of the National Labor Relations Act, and the Occupational Safety and Health Act).
4. The right to equal pay for equal work (the Equal Pay Act).
5. The right to overtime after forty hours of work in a week (the Fair Labor Standards Act).
6. The right not to be discriminated against because of race, sex, religion, national origin, pregnancy, or age (Title VII of the Civil Rights Act of 1964 and subsequent statutes).
7. The right to reasonable accommodation if disabled but qualified to do particular work (the Americans with Disabilities Act).
8. The right to 12 weeks of leave in any 12-month period because of a serious health condition (the Family and Medical Leave Act).
9. The right to free speech about union affairs, and to a minimum of due process when disciplined by a union (Title I of the Labor Management Reporting and Disclosure Act).
10. The right to pension security (Employee Retirement Income Security Act).

Most of these rights are discussed in more detail later in this booklet.

"WAIVER" OF STATUTORY RIGHTS

Collective bargaining makes it possible for working people to enforce rights through their unions. But collective bargaining sometimes takes away rights that workers would otherwise enjoy because of laws like those just described.

The leading example is the right to strike. Close to 100 percent of collective bargaining agreements contain a promise not to strike (and usually also, not to slow down or otherwise interfere with work on the shop floor, and sometimes, not to picket) during the life of the contract.

You might wonder how this is possible, since Section 13 of the NLRA stated explicitly: "Nothing in this Act shall be construed so as either to interfere with or impede or diminish in any way the right to strike."

The reality is that within a dozen years after passage of the NLRA in 1935 the right to strike was interfered with, impeded, or diminished in the following three ways:

1. In the very first collective bargaining agreements between CIO unions in auto and steel on the hand, and General Motors and U.S. Steel on the other, union negotiators agreed to prohibit strikes during the life of these contracts.[6] Such surrender or "waiver" of the

---

6 John Sargent, first president of the 18,000-member Local 1010, United Steelworkers of America, at Inland Steel in East Chicago, Indiana, makes the extraordinary assertion that workers there had more power before the union was recognized and before there was a collective bargaining agreement with a no-strike clause. "Without a contract, without any agreement with the company, without any regulations concerning hours of work, conditions of work, or wages,

right to strike during the life of the contract has become one of the two standard pro-management provisions of collective bargaining agreements (along with a management prerogatives clause that permits management unilaterally to close the plant).

2. In 1938 the Supreme Court decided a case called *Mackay Radio*. The Court distinguished two kinds of strikes: strikes prompted by the employer's unfair labor practices; and ordinary economic strikes. The Court held that economic strikers could be "permanently replaced," that is, that their jobs could be given to other workers to keep even after the strike ended.

3. In 1947, in Section 8(b)(4) of the Taft-Hartley Act, Congress prohibited secondary strikes and boycotts solicited by unions or their agents.

How do courts justify the abrogation of the right to strike by labor-management negotiators? The answer is twofold.

The courts often say: "You have the right to strike, but if you choose to give it away by ratifying a collective bargaining agreement with a no-strike clause, you have the right to give it away, too." This makes no sense because the ordinary worker has very little control over what goes into his or her contract. It is pure fiction to say that the ordinary union member has knowingly and voluntarily given up, or "waived," the right to strike.

The courts also often say: "It's all right to take away your right to strike because now that you have a union, you don't need to strike." The assumption here, which the United States Supreme Court has stated in so many

---

a tremendous surge took place.... Without a contract we secured for ourselves agreements on working conditions and wages that we do not have today." John Sargent, "Your Dog Don't Bark No More," in *Rank and File*, ed. Lynd and Lynd, p. 107.

words, is that Congress gave workers the right to strike and picket only to help them form unions. Once unions come into existence, according to this theory, workers should be prepared to let the union represent them rather than continuing to act on their own behalf. This argument, too, is erroneous because there is nothing in the legislative history of the labor statutes to justify the conclusion that the worker's right to concerted activity ends when a union is elected or when collective bargaining begins.

CHAPTER 3
THE BASIC LABOR LAWS

The basic labor laws will be found in the volumes of the United States Code. The Code is cited in the same way that cases are cited: 29 USC § 101, the citation for the Norris-LaGuardia Act, means, Title 29 of the United States Code at Section 101.

THE NORRIS-LAGUARDIA ACT (1932)

The fundamental purpose of the Norris-LaGuardia Act was to put a stop to anti-labor injunctions. In the early 1900s, when workers tried to organize the law was wholly on the side of the employer. Courts routinely issued court orders, called "injunctions," forbidding workers to strike and picket. The injunctions were usually issued on the basis of affidavits (sworn written statements) provided by the employer, without even giving the worker a chance to be heard. If the workers disobeyed, they were fined and jailed for contempt of court, without jury trials or other forms of traditional due process.

The key sections of the Act are Sections 2, 4, and 7 (29 USC § 102, 104, 107). Section 2 is a declaration of public policy. It declares that under modern economic conditions, "the individual unorganized worker is commonly helpless to exercise actual liberty…." To be genuinely free, the individual worker must be able to organize collectively.

Accordingly, Section 4 of the Act lists a series of actions that federal courts are flatly forbidden to enjoin (to "enjoin" something is to issue a court order called an injunction against it). No federal court may enjoin anyone involved in a labor dispute "from doing, whether singly or in concert ["in concert" means, together or collectively], any of the following acts":

1. Striking;
2. Becoming or remaining a member of a labor organization;
3. Paying strike or unemployment benefits;
4. Assisting a person involved in a labor dispute in a court case;
5. "Giving publicity to the existence of, or the facts involved in, any labor dispute, whether by advertising, speaking, patrolling, or by any other method not involving fraud or violence"—in other words, picketing;
6. Peaceably assembling. Section 7 of the National Labor Relations Act, enacted three years later, protects these same kinds of "concerted activity."

Section 7 of the Norris-LaGuardia Act sets forth certain procedures that federal courts must follow whenever they issue an injunction in a labor dispute. Essentially, Section 7 requires a court to hold a hearing and give each side a chance to present evidence before issuing an injunction.

Unfortunately, the courts have misinterpreted the plain language of the Norris-LaGuardia Act to permit federal courts to issue injunctions against strikes if the collective bargaining agreement contains a no-strike or binding arbitration clause. Courts will issue injunctions against some kinds of picketing as well. More about this later.

THE NATIONAL LABOR RELATIONS ACT (1935)

Another name for the National Labor Relations Act, or NLRA, is the Wagner Act. In the United States Code, the Act begins at 29 USC § 141.

The NLRA is the statute which, more than any other, regulates labor relations in the private sector. The NLRA created the National Labor Relations Board, which administers the Act. Domestic workers and farm workers are among the groups of employees excluded from coverage.

The philosophy of the Norris-LaGuardia Act was that if the courts could be kept from interfering, labor could fight its own battles. A few years' experience led many people to question this assumption. In 1933 and 1934, thousands of workers struck for union recognition, but often the result was bloody defeat. The drafters of the NLRA believed that labor would never be able to deal with capital as an equal without help from the government. The philosophy of the Act is that government must help workers to organize into unions, after which labor will be strong enough to bargain collectively. However, some organizations like the American Civil Liberties Union (ACLU) opposed the NLRA in the belief that it would give the government too much power over labor.

The heart of the NLRA, and the cornerstone of modern American labor law, is Section 7 (29 USC § 157). It states:

> § 157. Employees shall have the right to self-organization, to form, join or assist labor organizations, to bargain collectively through representatives of their own choosing, and to engage in other concerted activities for the purpose of collective bargaining or other mutual aid or protection....

What this has come to mean in practice will be discussed in Chapter 4.

Section 8 lists a number of ways in which employers are prohibited from interfering with the exercise of Section 7 rights. The most important sub-sections are:

Section 8(a)(1). It shall be an unfair labor practice for an employer to interfere with, restrain, or coerce employees in the exercise of the rights guaranteed in Section 7.

Section 8(a)(3). It shall be an unfair labor practice for an employer to discriminate in regard to hire or tenure of employment or any term or condition of employment for the purpose of discouraging membership in a labor organization.

Section 8(a)(5). It shall be an unfair labor practice for an employer to refuse to bargain collectively with the representatives of its employees.

Any person who believes Section 7 rights have been violated can file a charge with the NLRB within six months of the violation. Discharges, and similar problems affecting individuals, are usually filed under Section 8(a)(3). Problems connected with refusal to bargain, and unfair bargaining, are usually filed under Section 8(a)(5).

Section 9 creates a procedure whereby workers can select a bargaining representative. Because of Section 9, NLRB elections or card-check agreements have largely replaced strikes for union recognition.

THE FAIR LABOR STANDARDS ACT (1938)

The Fair Labor Standards Act, also known as the Wages and Hours Act or the FLSA, made labor's long struggle for an eight-hour day, and for the abolition of child labor, the law of the land. The text will be found at 29 USC § 201.

The Act prohibits the employment of children under the age of 16; requires employers to pay a minimum wage, which is readjusted from time to time; and obliges employers to pay overtime at one and one-half the regular rate of pay for all hours worked over 40 hours in a workweek. The Act covers private and public employers that engage in interstate commerce, but there are many exemptions. It is also worth checking the law in your state, as in some states the minimum wage is set higher than the federal level.

The Act is administered by the Department of Labor. Either the Department of Labor, or individual employees, can enforce the Act. If the amount claimed is not over a few thousand dollars, Small Claims Court may be a relatively quick option. An employee, usually represented by an attorney, may also bring suit to enforce the Act in either state or federal court. An employee may sue on behalf of others as well as on his or her own behalf, but each person on whose behalf suit is brought must file a written consent with the court. An employee who is successful in court receives any back wages due under either the minimum wage or overtime provisions of the law; plus an additional amount of wages as a penalty; plus a reasonable attorney's fee.

Suits under the FLSA must be brought within two years of the employer's violation, or within three years for a willful violation. If a group of employees join together in pursuing a back pay claim under the Act, their action may be considered concerted activity protected by Section 7 of the NLRA. *127 Restaurant Corp.*, 331 NLRB 269, 170 LRRM 1447 (2000) (employees joining to file civil action against employer regarding payment of wages were engaged in concerted activity). Similarly, an employer was found to have violated § 8(a)(1) by terminating employees who acted collectively in filing for unemployment benefits. *Tri-County Transp., Inc.*, 331 NLRB 1153, 171 LRRM 1031 (2000).

THE TAFT-HARTLEY ACT (1947)

From the day the NLRA was passed, employers tried to amend it. These efforts were finally successful in the generally reactionary climate that prevailed after World War II. The Taft-Hartley Act includes a series of amendments to the NLRA along with a new statute, the Labor Management Relations Act (LMRA).

Three provisions have been especially burdensome to workers' self-organization.

Section 14(b) gives state legislatures the authority to outlaw the "union shop." The union shop is the provision in many collective bargaining agreements that any new employee at a workplace where there is an existing union must join that union, or at least pay dues, within a certain period of time. Many state legislatures in the South and West have exercised the authority to prohibit union shop provisions.

Section 8(b)(4) outlaws "secondary" strikes and boycotts. Just as Section 8(a) of the original Wagner Act forbade various unfair labor practices by employers, so the Taft-Hartley Act added a new Section 8(b) which lists unfair labor practices by unions. When the workers of a "primary" employer go on strike, this provision is intended to prevent them from asking the employees of other companies for support.

Section 8(b)(4) is written in particularly foggy language. We will discuss in more than one chapter below various kinds of solidarity with striking workers of another employer that are still permitted.

Finally, Section 301 of the Taft-Hartley Act, 29 USC § 185, gives an employer the right to sue a union in court for violation of its contract. There was nothing inevitable about this amendment. In England, labor contracts were not legally enforceable until the passage of the Industrial

Relations Act of 1971, and when unions refused to cooperate with the law it was repealed in 1974. In the United States, however, thanks to Section 301 it has now become routine that when a union strikes in violation of the no-strike clause in its contract, the employer will rush into court and:

1. Obtain an injunction, despite Section 4 of the Norris-LaGuardia Act, requiring the union to stop striking and to arbitrate its grievances;

2. Sue the union for alleged "damages" (loss of money) caused by the strike.

One feature of the Taft-Hartley Act offers union members something positive: it protects rank-and-file groups that organize in opposition to an established union. Section 8(b)(2) of the Act prohibits a union from causing a union member to be discharged from employment so long as the employee does not fail to pay union dues.

THE LABOR MANAGEMENT REPORTING
AND DISCLOSURE ACT (1959)

The Labor Management Reporting and Disclosure Act, also known as the LMRDA or Landrum-Griffin Act, will be found at 29 USC § 402.

The LMRDA concerns itself with the internal government of unions. It was enacted at a time when Senator McClellan and other politicians were making a much-publicized investigation into union corruption and racketeering. The ACLU for years had pushed Congress to protect the rights of individual union members. And after Section 301 of the Taft-Hartley Act made collective bargaining agreements enforceable in court, it became critical for rank and filers to try to control the contents of their contracts.

The important parts of the LMRDA are Titles I, IV, and V.

Title I contains the so-called workers' Bill of Rights. These rights include:

Every member of a labor organization is guaranteed an equal right with every other member to nominate candidates, to vote in union elections and referenda, to attend membership meetings, and to take part in discussion and voting upon the business of such meetings "subject to reasonable rules and regulations in such organization's constitution and bylaws." Section 101(a)(1). A federal court has held that unless a union constitution provides for ratification of collective bargaining agreements, members do not have the right to ratify their contracts.

Every member of a labor organization has the right to meet and assemble freely with other members, and to express any views, arguments, or opinions. Section 101(a)(2).

Certain procedures are required before dues may be increased. Section 101(a)(3).

No labor organization may discipline a member for bringing suit against the union or its officers, provided the member first exhausts internal union appeal procedures, and provided also that no employer finances or otherwise backs the suit. Section 101(a)(4).

Finally, no member of a labor organization may be disciplined (except for nonpayment of union dues) without notice of specific charges, a reasonable time to prepare a defense, and a hearing. Section 101(a)(5).

Any union member whose Title I rights have been violated may bring a civil action in federal district court. As with all other provisions of labor law, what the Act provides on paper and actual results may differ.

Title IV regulates elections. Before elections, opposition candidates have the right to inspect a union membership list and, under court decisions made during the Miners for Democracy campaign, a right to equal exposure in the union newspaper. After an election, a candidate alleging improper election practices by a victorious opponent must first exhaust internal union appeal procedures for four months, and then may appeal to the Department of Labor. The Department of Labor can bring suit to set aside the contested election if it concludes that improper practices affected the outcome. But the defeated candidate cannot bring suit himself or herself.

Title V requires union officers to conduct themselves toward their members as trustees, that is, to avoid self-interested transactions and to report fully to the membership. This provision was intended especially to prevent financial misconduct but courts have also held union officers to be trustees in their other activities as officers.

The LMRDA also gives a union member the right to obtain a copy of the collective bargaining agreement governing his or her workplace.

THE CIVIL RIGHTS ACT (1964) AND
OTHER LAWS AGAINST DISCRIMINATION

Civil rights are protected by a series of statutes, some passed after the Civil War and others enacted in the 1960s and 1970s. They are collected in Title 42 of the United States Code. 42 USC § 2000(e), or Title VII of the Civil Rights Act of 1964, is the most important.

According to Title VII, it is an unlawful practice for an employer

> to fail or refuse to hire or to discharge any individual, or otherwise to discriminate against any individual with respect to his [or her] compensation,

> terms, conditions, or privileges of employment,
> because of such individual's race, color, religion,
> sex, or national origin....

Sexual orientation is not a protected class under Title VII but some states have laws that prohibit employment discrimination based on sexual orientation.

A charge must be filed with the Equal Employment Opportunity Commission (EEOC) within six-months of a Title VII violation.[7] (Note that this so-called statute of limitations is the same as for claimed violations of the NLRA.) There is an exception to the six month limitation when the violation is "continuing," that is, when it is not a one-time event like a discharge but a recurring pattern like a seniority system. However, in *Ledbetter v. Goodyear Tire & Rubber Co.*, 127 S.Ct. 2162 (2007),[8] the Supreme Court held that a woman who alleged continuing underpayment when compared with her male colleagues should have filed an EEOC charge within six months of the first act of discrimination.

You cannot go to court under Title VII until you first file a charge with the EEOC or with a state civil rights agency. After the charge is filed, the EEOC has six months within which to act. Because of its enormous backlog of cases it usually does nothing. At the end of this six-month period the EEOC must issue a "right to sue" letter if the person who brought the charge requests it, after which that person has another 90 days to bring suit in federal court. A plaintiff who is successful in court may be

---

7   If the complainant files first with a state or local agency rather than the EEOC, the filing period with the EEOC is 300 days or 30 days after denial of the claim by the agency.

8   Decisions of the United States Supreme Court are cited in three different ways: S.Ct. (Supreme Court), L.Ed. (Lawyers' Edition), or U.S. The U.S. citation is preferred but cases are often available first in the S.Ct. or L.Ed. series.

awarded reinstatement and/or back wages, plus a reasonable attorney's fee.

Although you have to file an agency charge before filing a Title VII action in court, you do not have to file a union grievance; and if you do file a grievance and lose, you can **still** go to court. The reason for these provisions is that Congress considers the right not to be discriminated against as more important than other rights. (How to prove a Title VII case is discussed in Chapter 4 under the caption "The Right to Equal Treatment.")

A worker who read a draft of this booklet comments: "Today, in construction, we sometimes find more protection as members of a protected group, i.e., 'over 40,' 'disabled,' or subject to 'sexual discrimination,' than we find in the NLRA. Many white, male construction workers don't yet know that their rights are protected by the EEOC."

OTHER LAWS

There are other important labor laws, such as the Occupational Safety and Health Act (OSHA), 29 USC § 651, and the Employee Retirement Income Security Act (ERISA), 29 USC § 1001.

However, if you develop a working familiarity with the six laws sketched above—Norris-LaGuardia; NLRA; Fair Labor Standards; Taft-Hartley; LMRDA; and Title VII—you will have the basic knowledge you need. They are like the basic contract. Other laws are like supplements, or memoranda of agreement, which add something to the contract but do not essentially change it.

CHAPTER 4

A RANK AND FILER'S
BILL OF RIGHTS

THE RIGHT TO ACT TOGETHER

It is strange, in our individualistic system of laws, to encounter a right to act together with others. Section 7 of the NLRA nevertheless proclaims a right "to engage in...concerted activities for the purpose of...mutual aid or protection."

These words reflect decades of legally unprotected collective struggle by working people. The heart of the labor movement—the reason that, with all its failings, the labor movement still in some sense represents a new society within the shell of the old—is the experience, forced on working people by necessity, that "an injury to one is an injury to all." Trade union officers sign their letters "fraternally yours." That they do so is a symbol, just as Section 7 is a symbol, of the reality of solidarity that underlies these outward forms.

As we've seen, the right to act in concert made its way into the law in the Norris-LaGuardia Act of 1932. Section 4 of that statute forbade federal courts to enjoin strikes, picketing, and the like. When the NLRA was young it was commonly interpreted to protect sympathy strikes and boycotts. Judge Learned Hand wrote in *NLRB v. Peter Cailler Kohler Swiss Chocolates Co.*, 130 F.2d 503, 10 LRRM 852 (2d Cir. 1942):

> When all the other workmen in a shop make common cause with a fellow workman over his separate grievance, and go out on strike in his support, they

engage in a "concerted activity" for "mutual aid and protection," although the aggrieved workman is the only one of them who has any immediate stake in the outcome. The rest know that by their action each one of them assures himself, in case his turn ever comes, of the support of the one whom they are all then helping; and the solidarity so established is "mutual aid" in the most literal sense, as nobody doubts. So too of those engaging in a "sympathetic strike," or secondary boycott; the immediate quarrel does not itself concern them, but by extending the number of those who will make the enemy of one the enemy of all, the power of each is vastly increased.

The right to act together is the right on which all other workers' rights depend. It is the enforcer, the working person's First Amendment. Acting in concert may take the form of union organization, but it may also take the form of shopfloor struggle in the absence of a union, or alongside a union.

SECTION 7 UNDER ATTACK

As one might expect, following the great upheaval of the 1930s the Congress, the National Labor Relations Board and the courts have done their best to limit workers' right to engage in concerted activity. This has been especially the case in the last few years when a Republican president has packed the Board with pro-business lawyers, but it is also a long-run trend.

For example, in workplaces where a union has been recognized, the Board and the courts tend to protect only concerted activity approved by the union. Earlier we explained that from the very beginning of the CIO, unions have been permitted to "waive" the right to strike by agreeing to no-strike clauses in collective bargaining. In a leading case at a San Francisco department store the union was permitted to give up the fundamental right to picket. There African American workers who considered themselves to be discriminated against asked their union to file a group grievance. The union refused. So the workers, when off work, set up a picket line on public property asking potential customers not to shop at the store until the issue of discrimination was resolved. The workers were discharged, and first the NLRB, and then the Supreme Court, held that their discharge was lawful because they should have filed individual grievances. *Emporium Capwell Co. v. Western Addition Community Org.*, 420 U.S. 50 (1975).

The powers that be have also promoted the notion that the right to act in concert is a "collective" right, belonging to everyone together but not to any one individual. A single worker's statement, "this is a hell of a place to work," was initially held by the Board to be an "indispensable preliminary step" to group action but was found by a reviewing court to be "mere griping," hence unprotected.

Likewise, the authorities have done their best to restrict activity aimed at defending class-wide interests, rather than narrowly-defined self-interest.[9] A strike protesting trade relations with Cuba was held to be unprotected, as was wearing a button with the words, "Dump Nixon."

Yet Section 7 remains a significant source of protection.[10] It has repeatedly been held that an individual's

---

9   A brilliant and comprehensive discussion of this assumption in labor law both before and after passage of the NLRA will be found in James Atleson, *Values and Assumptions in American Labor Law* (Amherst: University of Massachusetts Press, 1983).

10 Indeed, one of the authors has called Section 7's protection for concerted activity unrelated to a formal union the best-kept secret in labor law.

protest activity can be sufficiently linked to the general welfare that it should be considered "concerted."

Here are some recent cases. When an individual worker raised questions at a staff luncheon "on behalf of [himself] and other workers" regarding evaluations and the company's 401(k) plan it was held to be protected by Section 7. *Air Contact Transp.*, 340 NLRB 688, 173 LRRM 1429 (2003). A single employee seeking to enforce a right he or she "honestly and reasonably" believes is conferred by a collective bargaining agreement is engaged in protected concerted activity, even if the employee has his or her own interests primarily in mind and is mistaken as to his or her rights. See, for instance, *Temp-Rite Air Conditioning Corp.*, 322 NLRB 767, 154 LRRM 1017 (1996) (employee's objection to pay cut based on contract language was protected concerted activity); *Phillips Petroleum*, 339 NLRB 916, 172 LRRM 1433 (2003) (employee pursuing family medical leave); *Lance Investigation Serv.*, 338 NLRB 1109, 174 LRRM 1151 (2003) (employee seeking vacation pay). As we will see in a moment, when an individual worker's self-activity concerns health and safety it is especially likely to be viewed as protected by Section 7.

Similarly, activity on behalf of class-wide objectives has frequently been protected under Section 7. In *Eastex v. N.L.R.B.*, 437 U.S. 556 (1978), the Supreme Court held that Section 7 protected passing out a newsletter that urged workers to write to their legislators and register to vote so they could influence government policy on labor-related issues like the minimum wage. The Court said that the phrase "mutual aid or protection" is intended to protect workers when they engage in concerted activity in support of employees of another employer. Moreover, the Court declared, workers are protected by Section 7 when they seek to improve their situation by means other than union organization and collective bargaining. The

Congress that passed the NLRA "knew well enough that labor's cause often is advanced on fronts other than collective bargaining and grievance settlement within the immediate employment context."

This remarkable language offers broad protection to agitation on behalf of the working class as a whole and is still good law. Thus, an individual employee who told a person picking up an order for a newspaper where employees were on strike that he worked for a "scab newspaper" was engaged in protected concerted activity because use of the term *scab* amounted to making common cause with the Section 7 activity of the employees of another employer. *Office Depot*, 330 NLRB 640 (2000).

SEEKING SECTION 7 PROTECTION

Often protection is available to workers who frame their action so as to bring it within Section 7.

One of the authors was involved in supporting a strike by employees of a Buick car dealer. An anti-labor judge issued an extraordinarily broad injunction: he found in contempt of court one picketer who brought a cup of coffee to another, thus momentarily exceeding the number of pickets the court allowed at the workplace entrance. But dramatically effective strike support was developed nonetheless. At times in the week when sales activity was intense (such as Saturday afternoon) union members from all over the area staged "honk-a-thons," driving slowly past the struck workplace, signs displayed and horns blaring.

The following guidelines will tend to give you the best chance of bringing your protest activity within the protection of Section 7:

1. Act together.
2. If you have to act alone, tell management that you are acting for the other employees in your department or workplace, as well as for yourself.
3. If there is a collective bargaining agreement in your workplace, and what you're doing relates to any of its provisions, refer to it.
4. Even if your action concerns workers elsewhere, or a political object like legislation, the Board will be more likely to consider what you do protected if you show—preferably at the time of the action—how the action affects the working conditions of yourself and your fellow employees.

Often it appears that the employer administered discipline for more than one reason, only one of which involved concerted activity arguably protected by Section 7. In a 1980 case called *Wright Line* the Board adopted an approach later approved by the Supreme Court. In such "dual motive" cases the question to be asked is: Would the discipline have been administered anyway if the concerted activity had not occurred? For example, a worker supporting an organizing drive comes to work late one day and gets fired whereas a worker opposing the drive comes late but does not get fired. Other things being equal, you'll be able to prove that the union activist would not have been fired for coming late were it not for his protected activity.

THE RIGHT TO SPEAK AND LEAFLET

At the threshold of any concerted activity there is the need to communicate. The needed communication can take many forms: talking informally, speaking through a megaphone, writing and passing out a leaflet, wearing a button, posting a notice on a bulletin board, or holding a press conference.

There is what might be called a sacred contagion about such communication. One of the authors coordinated Freedom Schools in Mississippi during the summer of 1964. Later, as a law student, he read the case of *Tinker v. Des Moines*, in which the Supreme Court said that a high school student who wore a black armband to school to protest the Vietnam war was engaged in speech protected by the First Amendment and could not lawfully be sent home. He noticed that the Supreme Court repeatedly cited a case from a federal court of appeals in the South.

The earlier case turned out to be about the first day of public school in Fall 1964 in Philadelphia, Mississippi, the community where civil rights workers Chaney, Goodman and Schwerner had been murdered the previous June. On that day African American children came to school wearing buttons that said "SNCC" and "One Man, One Vote." They were sent home. The court said that was unlawful. Thus black youngsters in the Deep South made it possible for a white student in Iowa, a few years later, to protest a war.

BUTTONS

Workers have the right to wear union buttons and emblems anywhere on the job, during work time as well as during breaks. *Republic Aviation Corp. v. NLRB*, 324 U.S. 793 (1945). To negate this right, the burden is on the employer to show special circumstances, i.e., a button so provocative that it disrupts production. *Pathmark Stores, Inc.*, 342 NLRB 378 (2004).

Disruption is in the eye of the beholder. The first

editions of this booklet offered the example of a button that said "Ma Bell [AT&T] is a Mother": workers who wore this button were found to be unprotected when the telephone company fired them. Later some disgruntled steelworkers showed up at the office of the author of those first editions. Their strike had been terminated by the national union in a way that they didn't like. They wanted to wear T shirts that displayed a large screw over the word "Again." They were advised against doing so. The workers did it anyway and were never disciplined.

In general, excessive profanity or insubordination will cause buttons or emblems to lose Section 7 protection. In a 2007 decision, a nonunion construction firm did not violate the Act when it directed an employee to remove from his hard hat an emblem which showed "someone or something urinating on a rat that was apparently designated non-union."

When employees interact with the public as in a restaurant, or a hospital, employers are most likely to attempt to interfere with the right to wear a union pin. However, the Board has held that customer contact alone does not constitute the "special circumstances" required to prohibit union pins. *United Parcel Service*, 312 NLRB 596 (1993) (holding that a small union pin free of offensive messages did not interfere with the image of a neat delivery driver).

In jobs where workers are in contact with customers, the size and message of the union pin will be critically important in determining whether there is a right to wear those pins in public areas. Contrast with *United Parcel Service* the Board decision in *West San Diego*, 348 NLRB No. 24 (2006), available at http://www.nlrb.gov/case/21-CA-036384#documents (finding special circumstances justifying ban in public areas of a 2-inch square button stating, *Justice Now! Justicia Ahora!*).

TALKING UNION

Talking about a union or wages and working conditions is almost always protected activity, even when you're on the clock and in a work area. If your boss allows you to speak at work about things like sports or the weather, the boss must allow you to discuss the union as well as wages and working conditions.

"Soliciting," on the other hand, requires an immediate, active response from the listener. For example, simply inviting a worker to a union meeting does not rise to the level of solicitation. See, for example, *Wal-Mart Stores, Inc. v. N.L.R.B.*, 400 F.3d 1093 (8th Cir. 2005).

Asking a co-worker to sign a union card is quintessential soliciting. An employer may not prohibit soliciting that takes place during non-work time, that is, during a break or as you're leaving your shift, even if you're in a work area.

LEAFLETING

So long as one stays on a public sidewalk or right of way, leafleting is governed by the First Amendment. Unless restricted by a lawful local ordinance no permit is needed to leaflet on public property. The leafleter who takes reasonable care not to block the sidewalk, who does not become involved in incidents of violence, and whose leaflet is truthful, has the right to leaflet undisturbed. (Of course the police may interfere regardless of the law. The leafleter has a better chance to be left alone if within the foregoing guidelines, however.)

Once the leafleter leaves public property and enters onto the property of the employer, the rules change. If the employer is a **public** employer, then the First Amendment continues to apply, but speech inside the workplace may be more restricted than speech on the sidewalk because of considerations of time, place, and manner, or because it is considered to be disloyal.

If the employer is a private employer and engages in interstate commerce of any significance, then the NLRA including Section 7 is applicable. Here are answers to some common questions about Section 7 and leafleting at work.

Can I leaflet anywhere, any time? No, you may only leaflet in non-working areas such as the parking lot, locker room, break room, cafeteria, or outside the gate. Leafleting in working areas is unprotected even during non-working time. The theory is that such leafleting might cause litter that would interfere with production. However, if the employer allows workers to exchange documents unconnected with the job in work areas, it may not prohibit sharing written information in work areas just because the documents are union-related.

May I leaflet if I am off duty or laid off? Yes, but only in out of doors non-working areas, such as a parking lot.

Do union organizers have the same rights as employees to leaflet on company property? No. But union organizers who "salt" a workplace by going to work there in order to organize have the same rights as do other employees. Significantly, this means the employer cannot refuse to hire a salt because of his or her union affiliation and cannot discriminatorily fire an employee who has been identified as a salt.

Can the company call the police and have me thrown off the property for trespass? If you are on the property of a company where you work, probably not.

Creative and aggressive leafleting can be an effective way to remedy grievances on the job. In one instance, a Starbucks manager was really distinguishing himself as an enthusiastic union-buster and an overall jerk. Starbucks employees managed to take a photo of the manager and created a leaflet featuring his photo and a truthful list of the manager's abuses. The workers proceeded to hand out the leaflet to customers as they were entering the manager's store. It wasn't long before the manager kept his mouth shut and started behaving better.[11]

BULLETIN BOARDS AND E-MAIL

There is no legal right to use bulletin boards. However, if the employer allows non-company postings on the bulletin boards before a union organizing campaign, it cannot then prohibit workers from posting union materials once the campaign gets started. Also, if a union has bargained with the company for the right to use bulletin boards, it must allow rank and filers to post material critical of the union.

How would the Board treat employee communications on company e-mail? With the rise of e-mail as an indispensable mode of communication in many employment settings, unions and corporations were eagerly awaiting the Board's answer to this question.

In a gift to bosses just in time for the 2007 Christmas holiday, the Bush Board answered that employees do not have a statutory right to use a company's e-mail system for Section 7 communications. *The Guard Publishing Company, d/b/a The Register-Guard*, 351 NLRB No.

---

11 Don't let the legal protection for leafleting on the job on non-work time in non-work areas lead you to believe that such leafleting always makes good tactical sense. A common mistake new organizers make is to let the cat out of the bag about a union organizing effort by handing out materials at work where they inevitably come to the attention of the boss and trigger a union-busting campaign.

70 (2007), available at http://www.nlrb.gov/case/36-CA-008743. As with bulletin boards and other company equipment, the Board held that an employer could maintain and enforce an e-mail policy against all "non-job-related solicitations," including union solicitations.

After this ruling, an employer can allow workers to communicate freely about personal issues on company e-mail while forbidding communications soliciting support for a union, so long as the employer also bans the use of company e-mail to solicit support for any other group or organization. However, if the employer permits personal communications on the e-mail system or bulletin board, it will still have to allow Section 7 communications that do not involve solicitation.

PRESS CONFERENCES

In general, speech about workplace problems at a press conference or other public occasions is concerted activity protected by law. Workers should attempt to speak accurately and without unduly disparaging the employer's product.

Starbucks baristas in New York became increasingly fed up with having to work around rat and insect infestation. After multiple requests for the company to take action went unheeded, baristas blew the whistle at a press conference and shared video and photographic evidence of the infestation with the assembled reporters.

Following the press conference, baristas were extremely pleased to see senior Starbucks managers scrambling to make the structural repairs needed to cut down on the infestation. Because the baristas' collective speech concerned and accurately described their working conditions, Starbucks was unable to take adverse action against them.

If you need a case, the Board recently ordered reinstatement for a group of nurses who were fired after speaking to the media while on break about short-staffing. *Extendicare Homes, Inc. d/b/a Bon Harbor Nursing and Rehabilitation Center*, 348 NLRB No. 70 (2006), available at www.nlrb.gov/case/25-CA-028991.

MAGNAVOX

Section 7 law gives workers more protection to communicate than to act. A union **is** allowed to bargain away the right to strike. A union is **not** allowed to bargain away the right to distribute leaflets. *N.L.R.B. v. Magnavox Company of Tennessee*, 415 U.S. 322 (1974).

THE RIGHT TO GRIEVE AND BRIEFLY TO STOP WORK

"To grieve" is more than "to file a grievance." Filing a grievance is filling out a paper and giving it to someone else to do something about. To grieve is to express a protest. It can be effectuated through actions as well as through words; it will be more effective if it is not done alone; it need not be limited to matters contained in the contract; above all, it remains in the control of the aggrieved worker or workers.

Discharge or discipline of employees for grieving is generally held to be a violation of the Act. In the words of the Bureau of National Affairs' *Developing Labor Law*: "Assembling employees to present grievances, filing of grievances by employees [to protest sexual harassment] in a manner that bypasses the union, grieving under a collective bargaining agreement by probationary employees, and filing of numerous grievances, have all been viewed by the Board as concerted activity protected by Section 7."

When a group of employees stop work in order to present a problem to management it becomes a *de facto* work stoppage. In a case where workers refused to answer telephone calls for 20 minutes, the Board held that "when an in-plant work stoppage is peaceful, is focused on a specific job-related complaint, and causes little disruption of production by those employees who continue to work," employees are "entitled to persist in their in-plant protest for a reasonable period of time." *Benesight, Inc.*, 337 NLRB 282, 173 LRRM 1533 (2001), quoting *Cambro Mfg. Co.*, 312 NLRB 634, 636 (1993).

Brief work stoppages will be assessed on a case by case basis. A one-hour work stoppage in the lunchroom was protected, but a 12-hour stoppage held outdoors on company property was unprotected because of its duration. In *Bethany Medical Center*, 328 NLRB 1094 (1999), employees of a cardiac catheterization laboratory walked off the job 15 minutes before the first scheduled procedure of the day. The Board held that their action was protected because the routine nature of procedures scheduled for that day, the lack of emergency patients, and other specific circumstances indicated that the work stoppage did not create an imminent danger of harm.

Similarly, discharged striking workers were found to have engaged in protected concerted activity when they protested a supervisor's treatment of employees because the strike did not disrupt the employer's operation of the warehouse. *Rhee Bros.*, 343 NLRB 695, 176 LRRM 1357 (2004).

The briefer, the less disruptive, and the more closely tied to a danger on the job the stoppage is, the more likely it is to be protected.

THE RIGHT NOT TO CROSS A PICKET LINE

If there is no "waiver" during collective bargaining, employees who refuse to cross another union's lawful picket line are generally engaged in protected activity.

However, the right to picket like the right to strike may be waived, that is, given up. Some cases hold that such a waiver must be expressed in clear and unmistakable language, but others indicate that bargaining history and past practice can operate as a waiver even if there is no explicit waiver in the contract. Indeed a broad no-strike clause has sometimes been held to waive the right to picket unless evidence can be produced that shows the bargaining parties' intent to protect picketing.

A worker who honors a picket line later found to be unlawful or contrary to the picketers' collective bargaining agreement is at risk of being discharged. It is unlikely that the employer will be able lawfully to fire you outright. Courts will use a balancing test to determine the lawfulness of your employer's response. By balancing your Section 7 interests against the business interests of the employer, the court will decide whether the employer is prohibited from taking any action against you or whether you can be permanently replaced.

How is a worker who suddenly encounters a picket line in the course of his or her daily rounds—say, as a delivery driver—to know whether the picket line is lawful? The Board and the courts may not make that determination until months or years in the future.

All in all, this is one of those situations where one has to act first and hope that the law will be helpful. There are still some communities in the United States where people say, "Our family doesn't cross picket lines."

THE RIGHT TO REFUSE UNSAFE WORK

Second only to the right to equal treatment (see below), the right to refuse unsafe work may be the right best protected by labor law.

To begin with, Section 502 of the NLRA—which the Taft-Hartley Act did **not** change—states that "the quitting of labor by an employee or employees in good faith because of abnormally dangerous conditions" shall not be considered "a strike under this Act." Thus, a work stoppage over health and safety is not necessarily prohibited by a contractual no-strike clause. Thus also, this particular kind of activity is protected even if undertaken by a single worker.

The protection the Act gives to protests over health and safety is dramatically illustrated by two Supreme Court cases. In *NLRB v. Washington Aluminum Co.*, 370 U.S. 9 (1962), the Supreme Court enforced a Board order reinstating with back pay seven employees discharged for walking off their jobs without permission when they claimed that the shop was too cold to work. *NLRB v. City Disposal Sys.*, 465 U.S. 822 (1984), concerned a workplace where a collective bargaining agreement contained language about health and safety, and a single truck driver refused to drive a truck that he believed to be unsafe because of faulty brakes. The Supreme Court held that this was a protected act because it implemented the "concerted activity" of negotiating the contract.

Many more recent cases might be cited in accord with these two. In *Odyssey Capital Group*, 337 NLRB 1110, 170 LRRM 1387 (2002), employees engaged in concerted activity when they refused to perform work based upon the belief that the work exposed them to airborne asbestos. In *Magic Finishing Company*, 323 NLRB 234,

154 LRRM 1230 (1997), workers who walked off the job to protest unbearably hot conditions were held to have engaged in protected activity. In *TNS, Inc. v. NLRB*, 296 F.3d 384, 170 LRRM 2474 (6th Cir. 2002), it was held that Section 502 applies whether or not there exists a contractual no-strike provision and that workers who strike in a reasonable and good-faith belief that their working conditions are abnormally dangerous may not lawfully be replaced.

Note that these cases can be helpful in contexts unrelated to health and safety. They can be cited for the general proposition that walkouts by non-union employees are protected under the Act.

CUMULATIVE, SLOW-ACTING DANGER TO HEALTH AND SAFETY

As compared to a mine roof that may be about to come down or wire mesh through which a worker might fall to his death, the danger to health and safety posed by toxic chemicals in the workplace atmosphere presents a different kind of hazard. Cases like those cited above, or *Whirlpool Corp. v. Marshall*, 445 U.S. 1 (1980), the wire mesh case, involve **imminent** danger. The same is true of a Department of Labor Rule, 29 CFR [Code of Federal Regulations] § 1977.12(b), holding that an employee may refuse to perform an assigned task if "there is insufficient time, due to the urgency of the situation, to eliminate the danger through resort to regular statutory enforcement channels."

What if there is no immediate danger but conditions exist that threaten the employee with sickness or death in the long run, such as "black lung" among coal miners or "brown lung" in textile plants?

One of the authors experienced the possibility of affecting such situations without resort to government agencies or the courts. Four UAW members believed that workers were being poisoned by chemicals at an automobile assembly plant. On the basis of obituaries in the local press, they prepared what they called the *Lordstown Memorial* on which the names of former workers at the plant and their ages at time of death were written in black Gothic lettering. The display was made public at a press conference and attracted a great deal of media attention. The company and the union then did an epidemiological study which showed that a former worker at the plant was about 1.5 times more likely to die of cancer than a person in the general population.

Some time later, this author was driving through Warren, Michigan with the shop chairman at a huge Ford plant in that city. The shop chair pointed to the stacks on top of the plant roof that drew fresh air into the workplace. "Before, the stacks brought back into the plant the dirty air that was emitted," he said. "The company raised the stacks after you guys made that protest at Lordstown. We owe you."

THE RIGHT TO STRIKE

We have previously discussed the fact that the draftspersons of the NLRA sought to give special protection to the right to strike, but the courts, the Congress, and unions themselves have drastically restricted it. There is a poorly-defined right to stop production in order to protest oppressive conditions if the stoppage doesn't last too long and doesn't seriously disrupt production. The right to stop work over health and safety conditions, both in unionized and non-unionized shops, is presently the kind of strike that is most protected. Plant occupations are wholly unprotected by current labor law.

An important legal distinction exists between work stoppages triggered by an unfair labor practice and strikes in support of economic demands. If you and your co-workers do choose the strike tactic, you should always choose, if possible, to strike over an unfair labor practice and make clear that's what the strike is about. Economic strikers can be "permanently replaced," that is, discharged. In contrast, the boss must reinstate unfair labor practice strikers even if it means displacing replacements. *Laidlaw Corp. v. NLRB*, 414 F.2d 99 (7th Cir. 1969).

In most kinds of work (the health care industry is an important exception), workers need not give notice to their employers before walking off the job. However, economic strikers lose the protection of the Act when they strike to terminate or modify a collective bargaining agreement without complying with the notice requirements of Section 8(d).

Given the prevalence of no-strike clauses in collective bargaining agreements, an understanding of the scope of these provisions is critical. Sympathy strikes, whereby workers stop work in solidarity with fellow workers at the same company who are on strike, are not prohibited by a no-strike clause in the contract unless there is a "clear and unmistakable" waiver of the right to participate in a sympathy strike. *Children's Hospital Medical Center v. California Nurses Association*, 283 F.3d 1188 (9th Cir. 2002). A general no-strike clause will also not be held to prohibit a strike over an unfair labor practice, provided the ULP is sufficiently "serious" and the problem is not amenable to redress through a grievance procedure. *Mastro Plastics Corp. v. NLRB*, 350 U.S. 270 (1956).

Strikes are won when preparations are robust, solidarity among workers is deep, and strategy is intelligent. Legal protections for strikes should not obscure the tremendous challenge of carrying out a strike successfully. But when successful, there's nothing like the power of working people refusing to turn the wheels of production.

THE RIGHT TO BE REPRESENTED

The point of view of this little book is that the ultimate security of a worker comes from the willingness of those who work together to act together in solidarity. Yet there are times when one also wishes for the legally-protected presence of a steward or fellow worker as an advocate or witness.

Similarly, whatever problems membership in a sub-par union may sometimes present, it is to the individual worker's advantage that the employer should recognize and deal with whatever entity represents some or all of the workers on the job.

Finally, just as a client always retains the right to instruct and, if absolutely necessary, dismiss a lawyer, so workers must be able to ensure that they are not just represented, but fairly represented.

THE RIGHT TO THE PRESENCE OF A
STEWARD OR FELLOW WORKER

The Supreme Court has held that in a unionized workplace an employee has a right to ask for union representation at any interview with management that can reasonably be expected to lead to discipline. *NLRB v. Weingarten*, 420 U.S. 251 (1975).

A series of subsequent decisions have fine-tuned exercise of this right. Some of the ground rules are:

1. The employee must request the presence of a union representative. The employer has no obligation to inform an employee of his or her *Weingarten* rights. Nor can a union claim the right to representation on the employee's behalf.

2. The employee need not be sure that a requested interview will lead to discipline. *Weingarten* only asks you to have a reasonable belief. If the foreman says, "Come into my office," that should be enough.

3. If a union representative requested by the employee is available, the employer may not substitute another representative. But an employer need not postpone an interview because a union representative desired by the employee is unavailable for reasons for which the employer is not responsible, if another union representative is available.

4. The employee does not have the right to postpone a disciplinary interview in order to consult an attorney.

5. If the employer refuses to allow a union representative to be present, the employee may decline to take part in the interview, in which case the employer may proceed to impose discipline, or the employee may take part in the interview without representation. This may seem to gut the *Weingarten* right almost entirely when the employer is antagonistic to the union.

6. An employee may invoke his or her *Weingarten* rights and ask for union representation after an interview has begun.

7. An employee who has invoked *Weingarten* has a right to be told what the matter under investigation is, and to a pre-interview consultation with his or her representative.

8. Unless the employer fires the employee for the act of requesting representation during a disciplinary interview, a violation of *Weingarten* does not require the employer to reinstate a discharged worker with back pay. However, the burden is on the employer to show that discipline given an employee is not based on information obtained during an unlawful interview.

The question arises, in the typical workplace in the United States where there is no recognized union, may a worker insist on the presence of a fellow worker at an interview reasonably expected to lead to discipline?

The NLRB has gone back and forth on this issue. As this is being written, the Board with a conservative majority has answered, No. *IBM Corp.*, 341 NLRB 1288, 174 LRRM 1537 (2004).[12] However, under the *IBM* rule, the act of **requesting** a fellow worker as a witness remains protected even though the boss does not have a legal obligation to grant the request. It is worthwhile to bring a fellow worker to a disciplinary meeting and request that he remain for the duration of the meeting.

Invoking the right to request a witness will likely make the management officials present uncomfortable and help shift momentum onto your side. In the likely event that you are denied a witness, you can testify about that and management can be cross-examined in subsequent litigation. This way the judge might infer that management had something to hide.

---

12 There is an argument to be made that *IBM* leaves open the issue of whether *Weingarten* rights attach to workers in members-only unions not recognized by the employer.

THE RIGHT TO FAIR REPRESENTATION

Suppose, in a unionized workplace, the company violates the collective bargaining agreement. The member writes up a grievance but the union "forgets" to file it on time, or presents the case ineffectively, or takes the grievance through the first steps of the grievance procedure and then drops it before arbitration. Is there anything the member can do?

The answer is, Yes and No.

Under Section 301 of the Taft-Hartley Act, a worker has a right to go into state or federal court to enforce a collective bargaining agreement against an employer. But there's a Catch-22. On top of all the other problems connected with a lawsuit, such as expense and delay, to prevail in court the worker must show that he or she was "unfairly represented" by the union.

The Supreme Court has held that a union is guilty of unfair representation only if its conduct is "arbitrary, discriminatory, or in bad faith." Thus, for example, it is not enough for a union member to show that a grievance which the union refused to arbitrate was probably a winner. It must also be shown that the union had an improper motive in deciding not to proceed to arbitration: for example, that the grieving member belonged to a dissident caucus within the union.

The first editions of this booklet offered an extended discussion of the law of unfair representation. But it is very difficult for union members to win duty of fair representation claims, and we now think workers would be better off focusing attention on building organizations that really represent their interests.

It now seems to us that this convoluted area of the law is much less promising than the idea of minority or members-only unionism promoted by Professor Charles

Morris, discussed in the next section of this booklet. We should attempt to act on the idea of members-only unionism, for example by presenting a grievance as a group grievance that causes a temporary shutdown in production (see above), and by insisting on discussion and resolution of particular problems (such as the employer's failure to arbitrate a grievance) even before the employer is obligated to negotiate a complete contract.

THE RIGHT TO EQUAL TREATMENT

A sense of entitlement to equal treatment is universal among persons resident in the United States. When we feel passed over or singled out without good reason, we instinctively respond, "That's not fair!"

A first cautionary observation is that in order for unfair treatment to become "legally cognizable," that is, something the law can recognize, the person or persons claiming discrimination must be able to demonstrate membership in what the court call a "protected class." Nevertheless, the ongoing legal upheaval caused by the civil rights movement of the 1960s has resulted in protection for many vulnerable groups. Title VII of the Civil Rights Act of 1964 forbade discrimination in employment because of an individual's "race, color, religion, sex, or national origin." Later statutes prohibited discrimination based on age, pregnancy and disability. These categories are now all considered to be "protected classes."

The greatest problem in this area is not so much what exists on paper but enforcement. The administrative agency created to process Title VII claims, the Equal Employment Opportunity Commission (EEOC), has an enormous backlog. It is critical that workers keep in mind what they can do for each other. Whether or not a complaining employee is technically a member of a "protected class," steelworkers can look out for fellow workers approaching retirement, warehouse workers subject to quota requirements may insist that the quotas apply to groups of workers (with varying capacities) not to each individual, and a pregnant employee may be protected by fellow workers in a part of the workplace where supervisors rarely come.

The increasing use of arbitration agreements by employers represents another barrier facing workers seeking redress for discrimination in the courts. These employers require job candidates to sign contracts that prohibit them from bringing any and all legal claims in court. The worker must resort to an arbitration proceeding that often excludes important rights such as the right to bring a class action suit. See *Circuit City Stores, Inc. v. Saint Clair Adams*, 532 U.S. 105 (2001) (upholding the use of arbitration agreements in the employment context).

GRIGGS AND THE QUESTION OF INTENT

In every area of anti-discrimination law—schools, voting, juries, jobs—the courts have wavered as to whether the discriminatee must prove that the discriminator had an **intent** to discriminate. Intent is hard to prove. If intent is required, the civil rights plaintiff will win less often.

Generally, an intent to discriminate need not be shown in an employment case because of the Supreme Court decision in *Griggs v. Duke Power*, 401 U.S. 424 (1971).

In *Griggs*, the Supreme Court held that the employer's requirement that job applicants have a high school education constituted discrimination, when that requirement was not shown to be "significantly related" to performance on the job and had the effect of screening out African Americans at a "substantially" higher rate than whites. A Title VII plaintiff need not prove discriminatory intent but only discriminatory **effect**, the Court held. The Court stated: "The Act proscribes not only overt discrimination but also practices that are fair in form but discriminatory in operation." It also declared: "Under the Act, practices, procedures, or tests neutral on their face, and even neutral in terms of intent, cannot be maintained if they operate to 'freeze' the status quo of prior discriminatory employment practices." And still again: "Congress directed the thrust of the Act to the consequences of employment practices, not simply the motivation."

THE MCDONNELL DOUGLAS PARADIGM

The Supreme Court explained in *McDonnell Douglas Corp. v. Green*, 411 U.S. 792 (1973), how *Griggs* should be applied in a case where an individual claims a discriminatory refusal to hire.

1. The claimant should show that he or she belongs to a racial minority (or other group protected by Title VII); that he or she applied for a job for which he or she was qualified, and for which the employer was seeking applicants; that he or she was rejected; and that after the rejection, the employer continued to seek applicants for the job. This establishes what is called a "prima facie" (meaning, on the face of it) case.

2. Once the claimant shows the foregoing, the employer must present some legitimate business reason for rejecting the applicant.

3. If the employer appears to offer such a non-discriminatory reason for its decision, the claimant still has a chance to rebut that reason by showing it

to be a mere pretext. The employer's proffered reason for failure to hire (or administering discipline) may be shown to be pretextual if it has no basis in fact, if it did not actually motivate the employer's decision, or if the reason was insufficient to explain the action. *Manzer v. Diamond Shamrock Chems. Co.*, 29 F.3d 1078 (6th Cir. 1994). Pretext should also be found if the employer has previously tolerated the kind of conduct in which the employee (or applicant for employment) allegedly engaged, or treats the employee differently than other employees (or applicants) who engaged in the same conduct. *T. Steel Constr. Inc.*, 348 NLRB No. 79 (2006).

In many cases you will need to show that you were economically hurt by the employer's decision. There are some situations where you are not required to show economic harm such as loss of a job or promotion as the result of the employer's action. An unfavorable evaluation placed in your personnel file is illegal if based on race or gender even if it has not yet resulted in economic harm. Sexual harassment may be illegal even without an economic result because the discrimination itself is the injury.

APPLYING MCDONNELL DOUGLAS TO DISCRIMINATION AGAINST A GROUP

There is a similar procedure where a group claims to have been discriminated against.

1. A prima facie case is usually demonstrated by statistics. For instance, it might be shown that the population within commuting distance of the workplace is 35 percent black but that the work force is only 3 percent black.

2. Once the prima facie case has been demonstrated, the employer must articulate some business necessity for its decisions. Thus it might try to show that its business

requires a level of skill possessed by no blacks, or only a few blacks, in the area near the workplace. (The question could still be raised whether the employer should train minority applicants.)

3. Even if the employer appears to have justified its discriminatory practice by business necessity, the claimants may still rebut by evidence that the business need could have been met in an alternative, less discriminatory way. As an example, an employer might argue that there was a business necessity in its packing department for lifting heavy weights, hence it was justified in firing women unable to lift that much safely. The women might be able to counter by evidence that only some of the packages are too heavy for them, so that if the employer used men for heavier packing, women could perform the remainder.

One of the authors was co-counsel for a class action on behalf of African American "operating engineers." (Operating engineers drive heavy earth-moving equipment.) The suit was directed both against a class of employers and against the union, because union dispatchers were found to recommend African Americans for jobs of shorter duration.

In order to prove a prima facie case, counsel chose to examine the apprenticeship classes administered by the union. It was shown that some effort was made to recruit minorities as apprentices; that during the apprenticeship period the number of hours worked by minorities was not substantially less than the number of hours worked by whites; but that once African Americans or other minorities graduated from the apprenticeship program, their hours worked dropped off dramatically when compared to the work experience of Caucasians.

Finding that defendants could not rebut this prima facie showing of discrimination, the federal court ordered that union dispatchers send blacks and whites in alternation to jobs they were qualified to perform. Defendants were obliged to provide plaintiffs' counsel with their monthly reports to the pension fund as to the number of hours worked by each member of the union. Within a few years the percentage of total hours that were worked by minorities increased from less than 5 percent to over 12 percent.

But there is a sad sequel to this story, which is characteristic of efforts to change the system through lawsuits alone. Plaintiffs pleaded with the judge to recognize that minorities still lacked training on many of the more complex (and better-paying) machines. Experienced operators were in the habit of offering new white workers "seat time" to practice on machinery during lunch breaks and the like, but to deny similar assistance to blacks. Dispatchers could then plausibly argue that a black union member could not be sent out to work on a kind of machine that he or she did not know how to operate. No matter, the judge said: since blacks were now working a percentage of total hours that met federal standards, he would dissolve the consent decree. Within short order African Americans were again working in the neighborhood of less than 5 percent of total hours.

Litigation must therefore be accompanied by direct action, or the threat of direct action. In the region where one of the authors was employed, Burger King, a nonunion employer, hired few blacks and then mostly for jobs "in the back." A letter was sent to the employer concluding that claimants had no choice but to picket Burger King stores on Dr. King's birthday. A hiring agreement and an effective monitoring process materialized within a matter of days.

THE RIGHT NOT TO BE SEXUALLY HARASSED

The developing law on this topic distinguishes between two kinds of sexual harassment: so-called *quid pro quo* harassment; and the creation of a hostile work environment.

Quid pro quo is Latin for "one thing in exchange for another." A person claiming *quid pro quo* discrimination must show an obviously harmful action by the employer. The classic example is for a supervisor to make clear that an employee of the opposite sex who desires promotion, or a preferred job assignment, or a raise in pay, must provide sexual favors in exchange. And if the targeted employee refuses the advance and is demoted, otherwise disfavored, or discharged as a result, that is obviously a harmful action.

A more common but also more subtle form of discrimination involves the creation of a hostile work environment. Many kinds of conduct can create such an environment, especially if frequently repeated during a relatively brief time period. They include gross sexual language, touching and kissing, and the display of suggestive objects or pictures. Co-workers as well as supervisors can be held liable for creating a hostile work environment.

In any kind of sexual harassment claim, the employer must have been put on notice and be aware of the problem perceived by the complaining employee or employees. That is, the claimant must have made an effort to bring the problem to the employer's attention, awkward and even frightening as it may have been to do so. And if the employer responds with an investigation and appropriate corrective action, even if that corrective action does not resolve the problem, it may have a defense.

THE RIGHT TO BE FREE FROM THREATS,
INTERROGATION, PROMISES AND SPYING,
AND NOT TO BE RETALIATED AGAINST

The law allows employers to drown workers in endless anti-union propaganda. Indeed, management can fire you if you don't show up for one of its "captive audience meetings" designed to defeat your organizing aspirations. However, there are lines that the boss may not lawfully cross. These rules can be remembered by the acronym TIPS (Threats, Interrogation, Promises, Spying).

The employer cannot threaten you for exercising your Section 7 rights. Thus, "if you continue supporting the union, your pay will go down to the minimum wage" would be an unlawful threat.

Interrogation, or to be more precise, coercive interrogation, occurs when the employer or its supervisors seek to pry information from you about the union campaign or your own union affiliation. One of the authors responded to a line of questioning from several management officials about his role in a prior union action by objecting to the questioning as unlawful interrogation interfering with Section 7 rights. Needless to say, the tightly choreographed interrogation session for which the managers had hoped did not go as planned.

Employers commonly promise improvements to deflate organizing initiatives. Of course those promises never pan out once the organization is defeated. "Stop supporting the union and you'll get that promotion you've wanted" is a common and unlawful promise made by bosses and their supervisors.

Finally, the employer cannot spy or even create the impression of surveillance to stifle concerted activity. In the modern workplace, rank-and-file organizers must be vigilant against spying by the boss through surveillance cameras or through monitoring private e-mails.

RETALIATION

Close to a dozen different statutes provide for some sort of claim by an employee or employees alleging retaliation as a result of an attempt to use that law. Retaliation claims have certain common features.

First, the plaintiff must be an employee or former employee of the employer. A common example of post-employment retaliation would be a negative reference to another potential employer.

Second, the plaintiff must have been engaged in activity protected by the statute. Often this activity will be the filing of a claim or charge, or testifying in support of another employee who has done so.

Third, the employer must have subjected the plaintiff to an adverse employment action. In a recent Supreme Court case, the court held that reassigning the plaintiff from forklift duty to track labor and a 37-day suspension without pay were adverse actions. *Burlington Northern & Santa Fe Railway Co. v. White*, 126 S.Ct. 2405 (2006).

Fourth, the plaintiff must show that the adverse action was the result of the protected activity.

The fourth element is the most difficult to prove. The employer must be aware of the protected activity. Under some circumstances the knowledge of an agent may be imputed to the agent's superior. In general, the adverse action must have occurred in "temporal proximity" to (meaning, not too long after) the protected activity. Questions of mixed motive on the part of the employer—discussed previously in connection with *Wright Line*—and of pretext arise in the context of retaliation as well.

THE RIGHT TO BE RADICAL
NON-COMMUNIST PROVISOS

Openly expressing radical views in the labor move-ment is easier said than done. The subject is large and complex.

One of the obstacles to an activist who wishes openly to express radical views is the clauses in many union con-stitutions that deny union membership, or eligibility for union office, to certain kinds of radicals, vaguely defined.

Such clauses were typically added to union constitutions during the years just before, during, and just after World War II. In 1940 the CIO adopted a resolution stating:

> The Congress of Industrial Organizations con-demns the dictatorships and totalitarianism of Nazism, communism, and fascism as inimical to the welfare of labor, and destructive of our forms of government.

In the same vein, Article III, Section 4 of the constitu-tion of a major CIO union, the United Steelworkers of America, stated:

> No person shall be eligible for membership, or for nomination or election or appointment to, or to hold any office, or position, or to serve on any Committee in the International Union or a Local Union or to serve as a delegate therefrom who is a member, consistent supporter, or who actively participates in the activities of the Communist Party, Ku Klux Klan, or any fascist, totalitarian, or other subversive organization which opposes the democratic principles to which the United States and Canada and our Union are dedicated.

Laws passed by Congress sought to impose the same kind of restriction on freedom of association and belief. A clause in the Taft-Hartley Act as originally enacted (1947) required union officers to sign affidavits that they were not Communists before their unions could use the machinery of the NLRB. A clause in the LMRDA as originally enacted (1959) declared that no person who was or had been a member of the Communist Party could be a union officer.

The Supreme Court declared such prohibitions unlawful in *U.S. v. Brown*, 381 U.S. 437 (1965). Archie Brown was an open member of the Communist Party who had been elected to the executive board of his local union, and had official union backing. The Supreme Court held that mere membership in a political party is not a constitutional reason to exclude a person from union office. It struck down the offensive clause of the LMRDA.

A FIRST AMENDMENT ABERRATION

Public employees should be aware that the Supreme Court has handed down *Garcetti v. Ceballos*, 547 U.S. 410 (2006). This decision affirms previous holdings that public employees may be protected by the First Amendment when they speak as citizens about issues of public interest. (Thus a teacher represented by one of the authors engaged in protected speech when he spoke at a town meeting about matters of school policy.) But the Court went on to distinguish speech arising from an employee's workplace duties, declaring: "when public employees make statements pursuant to their official duties, the employees are not speaking as citizens for First Amendment purposes, and the Constitution does not insulate their communications from employer discipline."

In addition, courts generally hold that comments about wages or working conditions are not "matters of public concern," and therefore receive little, if any, protection.

LONG DISTANCE RUNNING

We offer it as our joint experience that radicals are most likely to survive in the workplace (and in the community) if they have been around for a long time and are regarded as capable and friendly persons.

Here is just one incident along those lines. When Gulf War I began, the Workers' Solidarity Club of Youngstown decided to picket against the war at noon every day in the downtown public square. The office of one of the authors was only a few yards from the designated location for picketing. As a member of the Club he participated almost every day. He did so with a sinking feeling to the effect that, "We've had fifteen good years here. But now we may have to leave town."

The response was instructive. At the time the author was assisting steelworkers and their families who were struggling to retain promised pension and health care benefits after employers shut down or declared bankruptcy. One man said, "You know I disagree with you about the war." Another man came up to the author on a sidewalk as they walked to a meeting in Cleveland and said, "You know I agree with you about the war." Then everything went on as before with both these individuals and with the group as a whole. The general sentiment seemed to be, "What else would you expect from Staughton?"

CHAPTER 5
PRACTICING SOLIDARITY UNIONISM

WHAT IS SOLIDARITY UNIONISM?

Solidarity unionism affirms the central role of rank-and-file initiative in workplace change. It stands in opposition to what has been termed "business" or "service-provider" unionism: the idea that a worker joins a union to obtain material benefits in exchange for monthly dues payments, much as the worker might buy an insurance policy.

In solidarity unionism, workers themselves carry out their own organizing. There are three fundamental principles: 1. Rank-and-file control; 2. Direct action; 3. Members carry their union membership with them, regardless of majority status, when they move on to other jobs (particularly important in high turnover sectors like retail or food service).

Business unionism is based on very different premises. In a business union: 1. The union is controlled from the top down by officers and staff (usually white males) who are not regularly employed at the workplace; 2. Direct action is avoided or used only when it can be choreographed and tightly controlled from above; 3. Membership is lost when the worker leaves a unionized bargaining unit.

Solidarity unionism offers an alternative. And, because solidarity unionism rejects the accommodation with capital inherent in the business union model, a solidarity union is situated to take part in the worldwide movement against corporate "globalization" and "neo-liberalism."

SOLIDARITY UNIONISM AND THE LAW

Because the goals and practices of a solidarity union differ significantly from those of a business union, a different legal perspective is also needed.

The business union is obsessed with the quest to become the exclusive bargaining agent for a particular bargaining unit. Only as a legally-recognized exclusive bargaining agent can the union bargain for a dues check-off clause. The way business unions win exclusive bargaining status is through a certification election conducted by the NLRB or a campaign for voluntary recognition by the employer, in either case driven primarily by outside staff.

Because exclusive bargaining status requires majority support, business union organizing focuses on getting signed authorization cards. All too often, signing that card may be the first and last union activity in which a worker will participate—even if the union wins! The worker is a passive spectator rather than an agent of change.[13]

Support from 50% of those voting, rather than a majority (50% plus 1), is worthless to the business union since it cannot result in a dues check-off. An election campaign that does not result in majority support is considered lost: the staff person, often recently imported from a college campus, checks out of the motel the day after the election; the business union sponsors no further activity at the workplace; and union supporters among the work force are simply left behind, exposed to discipline and discharge.

---

13 There is much talk in labor circles regarding the Employee Free Choice Act which, among other things, would compel employers to recognize unions when a majority of workers sign authorization cards. Regardless of one's position on such a legislative reform, it should be noted that it does not alter the authorization card-driven, staff-centered dynamic of a business union.

A successful business union campaign results in a collective bargaining agreement that gives up the right to strike and any voice in fundamental decisions about the enterprise, and directs the submission of grievances to a legalistic arbitration process. Workers are lulled into complacency for the duration of the contract, stirred into action temporarily when the contract expires, and then once again forgotten.

In the legal arena, business unions rely on the certification or recognition provisions of Section 9 of the NLRA. Solidarity unions heavily utilize the protection of collective action by Section 7, and the opportunity to file Unfair Labor Practice charges (ULPs) offered by Section 8.[14] Even then it is imperative that shop floor and community struggle not be diverted into the hallways of the NLRB. The serious limitation of ULPs, including lengthy delays, tragi-comically weak remedies, and inadequate substantive protections, must be frankly acknowledged to fellow workers.

It's particularly illuminating to consider how a grievance is remedied in a business union and a solidarity union. In a business union, when something goes wrong at work the union member calls a steward or business agent and hopes that some bureaucratic process disconnected from the rank and file will right the wrong. The worker is a passive consumer of a service and an individual spectator of a process under the control of others.

By contrast in a solidarity union, the worker shares his or her grievance with a committee of co-workers. They decide together on a course of direct action to right the wrong, which the workers will lead. The workers thereby

---

14 Once again, the authors refer to their pamphlet *Solidarity Unionism at Starbucks* (Oakland: PM Press, 2010), which explores the possibility of using Sections 7 and 8 of the NLRA while avoiding the representation process set forth in Section 9.

harness their own power and creativity rather than depending on "professionals."

Business unions sometimes say to members, "You are the union." In a solidarity union, that proposition is true.

THE NO-STRIKE CLAUSE, THE MANAGEMENT PREROGATIVES CLAUSE, COMPULSORY MEMBERSHIP, DUES CHECK-OFF, WRITTEN CONTRACTS, AND "MEMBERS-ONLY" UNIONS

Nothing in labor law requires a union to give up the right to strike, or to give management the right to make unilateral investment decisions, or to require all new workers to join the union, or to have dues deducted from the worker's paycheck by the employer. One of the authors and his wife interviewed veterans of the 1930s as to why CIO unions did not remain the unions they had dreamed of and organized decades previously. The old-timers repeatedly praised the process whereby a steward went to each worker on the shop floor every month to ask for voluntary payment of dues. That way, we were told, the member also had a chance to bring grievances to the steward's attention.[15]

Some local unions during the first years of the CIO embraced practices unheard-of later on. Sylvia Woods, an African American, said of the UAW local union to which she had belonged during World War II:

> We had the reputation with the international for being a good local. In fact, the region gave a party for our local because we kept 90% signed up....

---

15 *Rank and File*, ed. Lynd and Lynd (New York: Monthly Review Press, 1988), Introduction.

> We never had check-off. We didn't want it. We said
> if you have a closed shop and check-off, everybody
> sits on their butts and they don't have to worry
> about organizing and they don't care what hap-
> pens. We never wanted it.[16]

Ed Mann, three-time president of Local 1462, United
Steelworkers of America in Youngstown, Ohio, and
longtime member of the Workers' Solidarity Club of
Youngstown, had this to say about written contracts.

> I think we've got too much contract. You hate to
> be the guy who talks about the good old days, but
> I think the IWW had a darn good idea when they
> said, "Well, we'll settle these things as they arise."[17]

This doesn't mean that there can never be an agreement with the boss. Verbal or written agreements between
workers' organizations and employers are compatible
with solidarity unionism as a temporary way station to
workplace democracy. But workers need to decide for
themselves when it is helpful to have a comprehensive
written contract, when it is preferable to come to specific
agreements about particular problems "as they arise,"

---

16 *Rank and File*, ed. Lynd and Lynd, p. 126.
17 *The New Rank and File*, ed. Lynd and Lynd, p. 101. Ed went on to
say: "I believe in direct action.… You got to settle these things right
at the point of production, and RIGHT NOW!… If workers don't
sympathize, they won't engage in direct action. That's their way of
saying whether or not it's a good grievance.… Once a problem gets
put on paper and gets into the grievance system, you might as well
kiss that paper goodbye. The corporations saw this when they started
recognizing unions. They co-opted the unions with the grievance
procedure and the dues checkoff. They quit dealing with the rank
and file and started dealing with the people who wanted to be bosses
like them, the union bosses." *Ibid.*

and when it may be better to have no contract at all. Just which contractual provisions should be adopted and which should be off-limits also ought to be debated and ultimately decided by the rank and file.

The newest big idea in labor law is that "in workplaces where there is not yet a majority/exclusive representative, collective bargaining on behalf of the members of a minority labor union is a protected right" that should be fully guaranteed by the NLRA.[18] We think that this members-only strategy can be a stepping stone to solidarity unionism.

The organizer of a national members-only union of technical employees for IBM explains this approach in a leaflet for potential members. "Many employees have the misconception that all we have to do is call someone up and schedule a vote," he writes. But it's not that simple. For one thing, if the employer has workplaces all over the United States, it will predictably argue that the "appropriate bargaining unit" is regional or nationwide. Then a union with solid footholds in a few workplaces, but not in most, will predictably lose a vote.

The organizer of this members-only union poses the question, "So what do we do?" He answers as follows:

> We build the Alliance@IBM site-by-site, office-by-office, worker-by-worker. We organize for the long haul and when roadblocks are erected, we find a different path.
>
> One of those different paths is what is called a non-majority union.

This particular non-majority union has 400 dues-

---

18 Charles J. Morris, *The Blue Eagle at Work: Reclaiming Democratic Rights in the American Workplace* (Ithaca: Cornell University Press, 2005), p. 2.

paying members, scattered throughout the fifty states.

> Our message to our co-workers in IBM is that there is no need to be discouraged that we have not sought or won a union recognition vote through the NLRB. Simply put, we are a union as defined by section 7 of the NLRA and we will act accordingly. We believe that workers standing together can be very effective. In 1999 IBM employees in a revolt against corporate management changing our pension plan… held mass meetings nation wide, testified to congress and took other actions that resulted in IBM backing down and restoring choice to over 30,000 US employees.[19]

Another organizer, who is building non-majority unionism among adjunct teachers in universities, argues that "acting like a union" is the best way to go even when an NLRB election might be possible. "There is no point on which we cannot force concessions and some sort of de facto bargaining if we are strong enough," he writes, "just as our union ancestors did before the laws were passed." As soon as you have a serious committee you should consider "starting to act like a union," he continues.

> Do whatever sounds like fun and what people are willing to do. The employer will probably meet with you if you have a petition with a number of signatures on it. This starts the process of recognition and bargaining in fact, if not legally.[20]

19 Lee Conrad, "Organizing for the long haul. Building employee power in IBM," available at http://www.endicottalliance.org/organizingforth-elonghaul.htm.

20 Joe Berry, *Reclaiming the Ivory Tower: Organizing Adjuncts to Change Higher Education* (New York: Monthly Review Press, 2005), pp.

Legally-compelled bargaining with minority or members-only unionism will require a National Labor Relations Board different from that which exists as this booklet is being written. But we can begin to act out the idea right now, and it opens up several dramatic possibilities.

Even within a conventional strategy of seeking exclusive representation by a single union supported by a majority of workers in an appropriate bargaining unit, minority or members-only unionism would force unions seeking majority support to prove their worth through action instead of merely making promises about what they will do after union recognition.

Many of the problems associated with exclusive representation could be avoided if less than a majority of workers could lawfully require the employer to negotiate with them. At present, workers have few remedies for a negligent or inattentive union other than the nuclear bomb of decertification. Members-only unionism would make it possible in the United States, as in many European countries, for there to be more than one union in the same workplace, and therefore, "a wide choice of opportunities regarding the selection of bargaining representatives."[21]

WORKING TO RULE

"Working to rule" probably goes back to the workers who built pyramids in ancient

---

121–122.

21 Morris, *The Blue Eagle at Work*, p. 218. Nicaragua in the 1980s offered still another variant: At the expiration of every collective bargaining agreement, there was a new election to determine what union should exclusively represent the work force for the duration of the next contract.

Egypt. The boss seems to have more power than the worker. But the worker knows better than management how to do the job, and oftentimes the foreman, if required to do the job alone, is helpless.

Therefore the worker uses the supervisor's power against him. Whatever written rules exist are followed to the letter. All the informal shortcuts by means of which workers ordinarily maintain production are set aside. Output slows down as workers fill out forms, demand the availability of every tool listed in the employer's instructions, make unnecessary trips around the workplace, report mysterious machinery breakdowns, scrupulously follow safety rules, and otherwise act the part of half-witted but obedient subordinates.

Working to rule, or as it has also been called "running the plant backward," seems to have originated in modern times with the IWW in the early 1900s. In the era of globalization and plant shutdowns it enjoyed a revival that demonstrated both its tactical effectiveness and its strategic limitations.

SKIRMISHES

Beginning in the early 1980s, workers in UAW Region 5 in the Southwest won a series of victories by working to rule. Beside following management instructions literally, the workers at an auto parts plant in St. Louis, a Bell Helicopter plant in Texas, and elsewhere, together refused to work overtime.

Working to rule proved especially effective after the expiration of a collective bargaining agreement. In this situation, workers are no longer restricted by a no-strike clause in the contract, so that the full range of Section 7 rights to "concerted activity" become available. Under these circumstances workers may experience a joyous creativity: cell phones maintain communication between separate buildings, a whistle summons all within earshot to the scene of a confrontation with management, improvised forms of communication blossom. Since unions do not enjoy dues check-off when a contract is not in force, financial contributions like everything else become voluntary.

Traditionally when the contract expires good union practice requires "no contract, no work." But these workers, like workers at General Motors' Lordstown, Ohio plant in the early 1970s, found that staying inside the plant and engaging in direct action (what Lordstown workers called "the schmozzle") got better results than walking picket lines.

WORKING TO RULE AT A.E. STALEY

The most significant effort to work to rule came at the A.E. Staley plant in Decatur, Illinois. When the Staley contract expired in 1992, the plant was owned by a British conglomerate, Tate & Lyle. Under the NLRA, when contract negotiations are unsuccessful an employer can declare an "impasse" and legally impose its final contract offer. Tate & Lyle did so. According to two Chicago activists heavily involved in the Staley struggle:

> Tate & Lyle management virtually eliminated the safety program, gutted the grievance procedure, and weakened the seniority system. They substantially increased use of non-union contractors and raised workers' health insurance costs. Supervisors were given full latitude on work assignments and shift assignments. Tate & Lyle management quickly

evicted the union from its office in the plant and abolished "excused time" for union officers to handle grievances.[22]

Remarkably, the workers fought back.[23] Union meetings took place weekly and were attended by family members. During the nine months that they worked without a contract, 97% of the local union's members voluntarily paid their dues. A *Solidarity Team* was created to coordinate resistance in the plant.

Members of the Solidarity Team first reviewed the contract imposed by management, line by line, with every member of the local. Meetings were held in each of the four critical departments. Most Staley workers had more than two decades in the plant, often working the same job. Most of the supervisors had been installed when Tate & Lyle took over the Staley company in 1988.

The results were predictable. One twenty-four-year veteran recalled:

> You call up the boss and say, "This piece of equipment is doing such-and-such." And he says, "What do you think we ought to do?" And you tell him, "You come up here and tell **me** what to do. That's what they **pay** you for." And if he tells you to do something and you know it's wrong, you do it anyway.

This worker added, "Everybody knows you got to kick a

---

22 See Steven K. Ashby and C.J. Hawking, *Staley: The Fight for a New Labor Movement* (Urbana and Chicago: University of Illinois Press, 2009), p. 40.

23 The details that follow are drawn from Ashby and Hawking, *Staley*, Chapter 4. The authors also wish to acknowledge the insights of Rose Feurer, who at the time lived in St. Louis and was deeply involved in the Staley struggle.

Model A to get it to start. But it takes twenty years to know where to kick it."

On their own, workers began to meet at lunch, breaks, and shift changes, to plan their next moves. Grievances became group grievances. People started saying, "Let's get five other people and go see the boss," and the local's in-plant newsletter instructed, "Never go in one-on-one." The workers also created an underground weekly newspaper called the *Midnight Express*.

Within a few months, production dropped from 140,000 bushels of ground corn a day to an estimated 80–90,000. Unfortunately, under United States labor law the company had one major weapon left in its arsenal. On June 27, 1993, carefully choosing a moment (3 a.m. on a weekend night shift) when the number of workers inside the plant would be least, Tate & Lyle locked out the existing union work force.

AFTERWARDS

A "corporate campaign" directed at major stockholders in the corporation failed to provide an adequate substitute for work to rule. Even a hunger strike by Staley militant Dan Lane, and personal promises to Lane by newly-elected AFL-CIO president John Sweeney to support a product boycott, came to nothing. The Staley local joined a larger but ineffectual national union, a new local union president advocated settlement, a concessionary contract was ratified, and what had begun as a glorious uprising ended in defeat.

Certain reflections suggest themselves. One has to do with the company's readiness to resort to lockout. Like Staley, Bell Helicopter also responded to a work-to-rule campaign by temporarily locking out its work force.

However, as a defense contractor Bell may have been less able to sustain this strategy than was Staley, which processes biological feedstocks into sweeteners for soft drinks.

Further, when push came to shove the Staley workers decided against occupying the plant. One of the authors talked with locked-out union members who explained that they had selected the facility they wished to take over and developed detailed logistical plans for doing so. But the political support inside and outside the local union for this always-risky strategy was not available.

A final cautionary word about working to rule is also in order. The NLRB has held that workers are **not** protected by Section 7 when they decide for themselves what part of their work to do or at what pace they will labor. Work to rule is therefore a little like mass picketing: it works when you have large numbers and solid rank-and-file support, but without much help from the law.

THE POWER OF SECONDARY PRESSURE

66 **I**f it works, it's illegal," more than one labor lawyer has been known to say about pressure tactics against employers. But while it's true that much secondary pressure was outlawed by the Taft-Hartley Act, it's our view that a good deal of lawful and very powerful secondary pressure has been underutilized.

Secondary pressure is pressure exerted against an employer other than the employer with which workers have what's called a "primary" dispute.

For example, you work at a food warehouse and you're attempting to organize workers there. Your primary dispute is with the warehouse where you work. A primary employer has a major incentive to hold out during a struggle with its workers. On the other hand, a secondary employer has much less to lose if it complies with workers' demands. Thus a restaurant would simply need to purchase elsewhere the particular food products it has been ordering from the primary employer, the warehouse.

If you choose to exert pressure against a restaurant that sells some of the food that your warehouse distributes or a trucking company that delivers foodstuffs to your warehouse, then (unless the warehouse and the other employer are owned by the same entity) "secondary" boycott rules apply.

PRESSURE FROM THE COMMUNITY

First, we'll consider pressure exerted by worker centers,[24] community groups, students, religious organizations, and the like.

Taft-Hartley applies only to "labor organizations" as defined by the Act. Since community organizations are not "labor organizations" they can exert whatever secondary pressure they like.

In New York City, an employer brought an NLRB charge against a worker center called the Restaurant Opportunities Center of New York (ROC-NY). The employer sought to limit ROC-NY's picketing activities by casting it as a labor organization. In a 2006 advice memorandum, the NLRB General Counsel concluded that ROC-NY was not a labor organization and therefore was not covered by the various prohibitions in the Act as amended which apply to labor organizations.[25] The General Counsel was persuaded that,

---

24 Worker centers are membership-based non-profit organizations that provide assistance to low-wage workers especially in the area of legal rights enforcement.

25 *NLRB Office of General Counsel Advice Memorandum (Restaurant*

in contrast to a union's dealings with an employer, ROC-NY's interaction with the restaurant owners did not entail a pattern or practice that would extend over time.

A note of caution: If the support group is found to be an "agent" of the embattled labor organization, the group will subject the labor organization to liability. The issue of agency centers on control. A mere request for solidarity from a union to another entity does not create an agency relationship. See *International Longshoreman's Association v. NLRB*, 56 F.3d 205 (D.C. Cir. 1995).[26]

LEAFLETING AND PICKETING CUSTOMERS

Unions may lawfully call on prospective customers of a secondary employer to boycott the secondary's **entire** establishment if they do so only through leaflets. *DeBartolo Corp. v. Fla. Gulf Coast Trades Council (DeBartolo II)*, 485 U.S. 568 (1998).

What union leafleters may not legally do is to induce a strike of the secondary employer's workers or block deliveries to the secondary. As a safeguard, note on the leaflet that these are not your objectives and that your labor dispute is with the primary employer.

Picketing that targets the employees of a secondary employer is prohibited by Section 8(b)(4). Picketed directed at customers of a secondary employer is restricted but not wholly prohibited. A landmark Supreme Court decision, and cases following it, carve out the guidelines

---

Opportunities Center of New York), 2-CP-1067 (2006), available at www.nlrb.gov/case/02-CP-001067.

26 The latest flavor of the month for anti-union lawyers and their clients is filing lawsuits against unions and worker support groups under the preposterous theory that they form unlawful conspiracies under the Racketeer Influenced and Corrupt Organizations Act (RICO).

for lawful secondary picketing. *NLRB v. Fruit Packers (Tree Fruits)*, 377 U.S. 58 (1964).

The key is to identify the particular product of the primary employer that pickets ask customers of the secondary employer not to purchase. In *Tree Fruits*, for example, picket signs were held to be lawful because they solicited a boycott of Washington State apples and did not call for a boycott of the entire Safeway store where the apples were sold.

Be careful, though, if the secondary employer derives nearly all its revenue from the products of the primary employer. The Supreme Court has held that under those circumstances even picketing directed solely at products of the primary employer is unlawfully coercive.

What about using the beloved inflatable rat at a secondary's location? The issue is whether the rat is more like speech or more like a picket. Judges have gone both ways and, as we write, the NLRB has declined to resolve the matter. If you want to use a rat outside the workplace of a secondary employer, you can minimize the likelihood of liability by: clearly directing your message to customers; using the rat when customers, not just workers, are in evidence at the site; and refraining from patrolling (picketing) back and forth beside the rat. A banner displaying a rat is a less risky alternative.

Finally, whatever medium one chooses for conveying a message at the workplace of a secondary employer, the message must be truthful.

USING WAGE AND HOUR CLAIMS

Worker centers have made good use of wage claims on behalf of workers who are paid less than federal and state law requires.

As previously discussed, the federal Fair Labor Standards Act (the FLSA, or Wages and Hours law) requires the payment of a minimum hourly wage plus time and a half that minimum wage for "overtime," that is, hours more than forty worked in a workweek. The FLSA also includes stronger protection against retaliation than does the NLRA.

FEDERAL AND STATE CLAIMS

It's critical for solidarity union organizers to stress that lawsuits play merely a secondary role to worker organizing on the shop floor and not to overstate the efficacy of legal action. That said, let's take a look at how best to deploy a wage and hour lawsuit.

The employer's potential liability in a wages and hours case is maximized if its violation is "willful." For willful violations, employees may double the lost earnings to which they are entitled. 29 U.S.C. § 216. In addition, proving a willful violation enables employees to collect three years of lost wages instead of just two. 29 U.S.C. § 255. A willful violation is made out by showing that the employer knowingly or recklessly disregarded FLSA violations. *McLaughlin v. Richland Shoe Co.*, 486 U.S. 128 (1988), applied for example in *Reich v. Waldbaum, Inc.*, 52 F.3d 35 (2d Cir. 1995).

If the employer retaliates against workers who file under the FLSA, the employee is authorized to add punitive damages (in effect, a monetary penalty) to back pay owed. A federal judge also has the power to issue an injunction against further retaliation.

Under the collective action provision of the FLSA, 29 U.S.C. § 216(b), each worker who wishes to join a suit must "opt-in" by signing a simple form.

Many states also have their own wages and hours laws, which may be more protective than federal law. In some of those jurisdictions workers can file for lost wages as a class. Members of a class such as "all full-time wage workers for corporation X in location Y during time period Z" then are automatically covered unless they choose to "opt-out."

State claims, whether or not brought as a class action, sometimes have added benefits such as a longer period in which to file the claim, a higher minimum wage, and greater monetary damages.

When workers bring a federal lawsuit under the FLSA, they can file related state claims as well under the law of supplemental or "pendant" jurisdiction. 28 U.S.C. § 1367. In some parts of the country, workers can bring a federal collective action and a state class action in the same case. *Lindsay v. Gilco*, 448 F.3d 416 (D.C. Cir. 2006).

Advocates for undocumented immigrant workers are well aware of the unfortunate Supreme Court decision in the *Hoffman Plastic* case (discussed below). While *Hoffman* has restricted available remedies for certain undocumented employees under the NLRA, these workers are still covered by the wage and hour laws. See *Zavala v. Wal-Mart Stores, Inc.*, 393 F.Supp.2d 295 (D.N.J. 2005).

SAVING FRINGE BENEFITS

It is somewhat bizarre to use the term "fringe benefits" to describe pensions and especially health insurance for retirees. Many retirees have been permanently laid off before attaining the age of eligibility for Medicare and are wholly dependent on collectively bargained health insurance.

When LTV Steel declared bankruptcy in July 1986 and simultaneously cut off health insurance for retirees, Roy St. Clair had just been released from a Youngstown, Ohio hospital. He experienced a recurrence of heart symptoms but did not seek to re-enter the hospital because he did not know how he could pay for it. Instead he frantically sought replacement insurance. Mr. St. Clair died the next day.[27]

Almost all other industrialized nations provide retirement benefits as government programs financed by taxation. In the United States, pensions and health insurance became part of collective bargaining contracts during and just after World War II. Wartime regulations, and the promises of union leaders to "freeze" wage demands, made it impossible for workers to pursue wage increases to keep up with inflation in the cost of living. Fringe benefits came to be negotiated as a substitute. Workers viewed these promised benefits as deferred compensation that would make possible a trouble-free retirement.

When the war ended, the manufacturing plants of Germany and Japan lay in ruins and it seemed that companies headquartered in the United States would enjoy a virtual monopoly in supplying worldwide markets for the indefinite future.

It proved otherwise. By the 1960s competitors abroad had rebuilt their facilities with the most up-to-date technology. In steel, for example, competitors installed basic oxygen furnaces and electric furnaces to melt iron ore and other ingredients into steel at a time when U.S. Steel built a new complex in Pennsylvania with outmoded open hearth furnaces.

---

27 This subject is more fully presented in Staughton and Alice Lynd, "Labor Law in the Era of Multinationalism: The Crisis in Bargained-For Fringe Benefits," 93 *West Virginia Law Review* No. 4 (Summer 1991), pp. 907–44.

As importation into the United States of products made abroad increased, and responsive technological steps in the United States increased productivity per "man hour," the ratio of retirees to active workers in steel and auto firms increased also. It began to become awkward or impossible to pay three or four retirees their promised fringe benefits from the surplus value created by a single production worker. This is the problem of "legacy costs" that is at the heart of the crisis in fringe benefits.

NO LEGAL RELIEF

Labor law and the law under ERISA (the Employee Retirement Income Security Act) provide inadequate remedies.

First, employers are not required by law to bargain over retiree benefits.

Second, union negotiators have often permitted companies to insert language in contract provisions for retiree health care benefits that allow the employer to change these provisions unilaterally.

Third, federal law enables corporations to "terminate" some kinds of pension obligations by transferring payment of basic benefits to the government, but there are no comparable provisions for health benefits.

Fourth, federal bankruptcy judges allow employers in bankruptcy proceedings to pay off "secured" creditors such as banks before meeting their obligations to retirees.[28]

---

28 The Retiree Benefit Bankruptcy Protection Act of 1988 directs a Chapter 11 debtor-in-possession to "timely pay and...not modify" retiree medical benefits unless a modification is negotiated with a union (in the case of hourly retirees) or ordered by the court. 11 U.S.C. § 1114(e)(1) (1989). The experience of one of the authors is that, in practice, federal bankruptcy courts permit bankrupt companies to pay off banks and other secured creditors before attending to promises made to retirees.

Fifth, federal bankruptcy law leaves it up to the union whether or not it will represent individual retirees in bankruptcy court.[29] This arrangement is unfortunate because retirees in most unions do not pay dues, do not vote for union officers, and do not have an opportunity to ratify or reject contracts.

As a result, the union has a conflict of interest if it seeks to represent both active members and retirees, and will inevitably tend to favor its dues-paying active members. A union that bargains for both current workers and retirees may be compared to the union of white railroad workers that sought to bargain away the rights of black workers who were not allowed in the union and could not vote on contracts. *Steele v. Louisville & Nashville Railroad*, 323 U.S. 192 (1944).

SOLIDARITY USA

What can retirees do to protect themselves? As in so many arenas of solidarity unionism, the answer is not to seek a legal solution but to use those legal protections that are available to seek a solution through direct action.

After LTV Steel declared bankruptcy in the summer of 1986, the wife of an LTV steel retiree called radio talk shows to announce a meeting in downtown Youngstown the next Saturday afternoon. A thousand people attended. In a follow-up meeting, it was suggested from the floor that we were something like Polish Solidarity, which had recently been in the news. The new organization adopted the name *Solidarity USA*.[30]

---

29 A union is permitted to choose whether or not it will represent retirees in bankruptcy proceedings. 11 U.S.C. § 1114(c)(1) (1989).

30 See Alice and Staughton Lynd, "'We Are All We've Got': Building a Retiree Movement in Youngstown, Ohio," in *Law Stories*, ed. Gary

Even the conservative local press condemned LTV's sudden, unilateral termination of benefits as heartless. Less than a month after it stopped paying benefits, LTV asked the Bankruptcy Court for permission to resume payments.

In subsequent agitation, Solidarity USA adopted the practice of informing a corporation, union, or insurer (including LTV Steel, the United Steelworkers of America, and Blue Cross) that it would appear on a designated day and expect to confer with representatives of the chosen interlocutor. Were it not possible to confer, we told them, we would just picket outside the front door.

We were never denied entrance. Without fail a representative of the beleaguered entity within would appear and invite "your lawyers" or "your leaders" to a meeting, sometimes specifying how many persons might take part. We always answered, "No, we have a committee. We want you to hear from people who actually lost their benefits."

Because of many, many early-morning and late-night bus rides, by our calculation when LTV Steel emerged from bankruptcy its retirees had regained roughly the same benefits they were receiving when the company sought bankruptcy protection.

THE FIGHT AGAINST SHUTDOWNS

Since this booklet was first published (1978, with a revised edition in 1982) the central economic fact in the lives of many American workers has been plant shutdowns, especially in the "Rust Belt" of the Midwest.

There had been previous waves of factory closings: think of the shuttered textile mills along the streams

Bellow and Martha Minow (Ann Arbor: University of Michigan Press, 1996), pp. 77–99.

that run through many cities in New England. In the past, companies that left town typically relocated to the Southern United States. Nowadays they more often move out of the country.

The trade union movement has had no effective response to plant shutdowns. The major obstacles have been: 1. the "management prerogative" clause in almost all collective bargaining agreements negotiated after World War II that permits companies to make unilateral investment decisions; and 2. court cases which hold that company investment and shutdown determinations are at the "core of entrepreneurial control" and, for that reason, are not a mandatory subject of bargaining. It is unlawful for a union to strike over a non-mandatory subject of bargaining.

As the result of manufacturing plant shutdowns, service industries that cannot move—medical care, education, food and building services, local utilities, construction, trucking—have, in general, offered the only realistic possibilities for union organization. This fact prompted seven major unions in such industries to break away from the AFL-CIO in 2005 to form the Change to Win federation.

WHY DON'T WE BUY THE DAMN PLACE?

One response of manufacturing workers and their unions has been to explore worker-community purchase and operation. This strategy often took the form of an Employee Stock Ownership Plan, or ESOP. Basically, what happens in an ESOP is that employees give up a portion of their wages and accept stock in the company as a substitute. In theory this may provide a firm with sufficient working capital to stay in business.

With rare exceptions, ESOPs have been successful only in small- and medium-size companies and offer only a temporary strategy for responding to a proposed plant shutdown. In some ESOPs, union officers have become board members of the worker-owned entity. Experience suggests that this scenario presents a conflict of interest: it seems wiser for one group of persons to represent employees as workers concerned with wages, benefits, and health and safety, and another group of persons to represent employees as owners or part-owners of a company seeking to stay in business.

In Youngstown, Pittsburgh and a few other places, it was proposed that municipalities could acquire plants threatened with closure by using the eminent domain power. Lawful exercise of eminent domain requires two things: a public purpose, which is usually obvious; and sufficient capital to pay the present owner "fair market value," which is almost never available. The mere threat of eminent domain has been effective in some instances, as at a NABISCO plant in Pittsburgh when the mayor threatened to bake his own Oreo cookies if the company followed through on its announced decision to relocate.

A variation on the theme of worker-community ownership has been litigation seeking to make companies perform past promises to the community or the union. In Ypsilanti, Michigan, a local judge found that General Motors was bound by a promise to keep the plant open, but his decision was overturned on appeal.

Finally, speaking and leafleting about saving your plant may be considered unprotected by the NLRB. The Board has held that advocacy of an Employee Stock Ownership Plan to buy out the employer is not protected by Section 7 since the proposal did not "advance employees' interests as employees, but rather advances employees' interests as entrepreneurs, owners, and managers."

SIT-INS AND OCCUPATIONS

Because all other strategies have been unsuccessful, workers think about sitting-in and occupying the plant. They perceive that if they can prevent the company from moving the machinery, there remains a possibility that production will resume and their jobs will be saved.

Between 1936 and 1939 American workers staged 583 sit-down strikes that lasted at least one day.[31] Certain sympathetic law professors made a determined effort to argue that at least under some circumstances, for example when the employer had committed outrageous unfair labor practices, a sit-in might be lawful. But in *NLRB v. Fansteel Metallurgical Corp.*, 306 U.S. 240 (1939), the Supreme Court said, No: henceforth, no matter what the employer might have done to provoke the situation, a sit-in or plant occupation was unlawful trespass for which an employee might be lawfully discharged.

In other countries, usually in much smaller workplaces, plant occupations have sometimes been successful. In Argentina, for example, workers at print shops, at health clinics, at a ceramics factory, at a butchery, even at a hotel, have "recuperated" their places of work when the owners abandoned them or fell far behind in paying wages.[32]

In this country, workers who opt for sitting-in or occupation must begin with the recognition that they are acting outside the law. That doesn't mean that such actions are hopeless or should never be undertaken. What it means is that, as is true even in Argentina, everything will depend

---

31 James Gray Pope, "Worker Lawmaking, Sit-Down Strikes, and the Shaping of American Industrial Relations, 1935–1958," *Law and History Review*, v. 24, no. 1 (Spring 2006), p. 45.

32 Inspiring first-hand accounts are collected in Marina Sitrin ed., *Horizontalism: Voices of Popular Power in Argentina* (Oakland: AK Press, 2006), pp. 67–105.

in the end on the ability of the workers to persuade the immediate neighborhood and the larger community that they are acting justly, and that it would be cruel and unfair to permit the legal owner to take their jobs away.

NO ONE IS ILLEGAL

No human being is illegal. We are far stronger if we stand together instead of letting bosses and politicians divide us.

While the law does erect hurdles to immigrant organizing and often treats immigrants like second-class workers, it is possible to build solidarity regardless of immigration status. Indeed, much of the growth in the labor movement is taking place among immigrant workers.

HOFFMAN PLASTIC

The landmark Supreme Court case in the area of undocumented immigrants and labor organizing is *Hoffman Plastic Compounds, Inc. v. NLRB*, 535 U.S. 137 (2002). In that case, a worker named Jose Castro supported an organizing drive at a plastics factory and was active in encouraging his fellow workers to sign up with the union. In retaliation, the company fired him along with other pro-union employees. Castro was an undocumented worker from Mexico and had shown fraudulent papers to obtain the job.

In 2002, thirteen years after Jose was fired, the Supreme Court decided his case. The Court held, in an opinion by then-Chief Justice Rehnquist, that Jose had been illegally fired but was not entitled to back pay. Rehnquist argued that immigration law trumped this particular

NLRA remedy. He maintained that even in the absence of back pay, "significant sanctions" against Hoffman had been imposed. The significant sanctions were: a piece of paper posted on the wall for ninety days which said that Hoffman would not again fire union supporters, and a **highly** improbable contempt order should the illegal conduct be repeated.

Hoffman is no doubt a terrible decision but a solidarity union can and must overcome it. You'll see how to get around *Hoffman* by looking at what the decision did **not** do.

First, *Hoffman* did not take away from undocumented workers their status as "employees" under the NLRA. Therefore, undocumented workers still have the absolute Section 7 right to organize and to join unions, and retaliation for that activity remains illegal. This undisturbed right to join a union is critical for workers to understand, especially if the employer's union-busting campaign makes the common but erroneous argument to the contrary.

Second, as Justice Breyer pointed out in his dissent, *Hoffman* did not involve an employer who **knowingly** hires an undocumented worker as is often the case in industries employing large numbers of immigrants. Justice Breyer's dissent was the basis for the first case after *Hoffman* to distinguish *Hoffman* and order back pay for undocumented workers who were illegally fired. *Mezonos Maven Bakery*, Case No. 29-CA-25476 (2006), available at http://www.nlrb.gov/case/29-CA-025476.

In *Mezonos Bakery*, a group of seven undocumented employees who were not members of a labor union complained about disrespectful treatment from a supervisor. Such concerted activity is protected by the NLRA. Nonetheless, the boss illegally discharged the employees.

The employer sought to rely on *Hoffman* in order to avoid back pay. However, unlike Jose Castro in *Hoffman*, the bakery workers had never been asked to show immigration papers. Administrative Law Judge Steven Davis held that the concerns expressed in *Hoffman* were not implicated in a case where the employer was fully aware that the employees did not have immigration papers. Judge Davis ordered that the workers be paid the money they would have earned had they not been illegally fired.

The same logic was applied in the union organizing context in *Handyfat Trading, Inc.*, Case No. 29-CA-28181, available at http://www.nlrb.gov/case/29-CA-028181. *Handyfat* relied on *Mezonos* and ordered back pay and reinstatement for nine undocumented IWW food warehouse workers who had never shown false immigration papers and who were fired as a group for joining the union. As we write, both the *Mezonos* and *Handyfat* decisions have been appealed.

Finally: 1. Nothing in *Hoffman* prevents unions, workers' centers, and community groups from deploying the full array of their own direct action tools in support of undocumented workers; 2. As in other law enforcement settings, potential discriminatees should be advised not to discuss their immigration status with government agents.

OTHER BATTLES, OTHER LAWS

In addition to the right to join a union protected by the NLRA, undocumented employees are also covered by minimum wage and overtime laws, by the safety standards contained in OSHA, and in most jurisdictions, by the workers' compensation system and Title VII.

Employer sanctions contained in Section 274 of the Immigration and Nationality Act of 1986 make it illegal for employers knowingly to employ undocumented workers. Some employers try to use this provision to smash organizing efforts.

Many employers, when hiring a worker, fail to obtain the I-9 forms required by the law. Some employers even instruct new employees as to how to obtain fraudulent papers. Then, if the newly-hired workers engage in organizing activity, the boss tries to retaliate by demanding that workers verify their immigration status.

Sometimes employers will even call in an audit from Immigration and Customs Enforcement (ICE). These audits can lead to terrifying immigration raids and the mere threat of such a raid is often enough to stop an organizing effort in its tracks.

Employers also use what are called Social Security "no-match letters" to try to stifle immigrant organizing. The Social Security Administration sends a no-match letter to an employer when an employee's Social Security number does not correspond with the Administration's data base.

Employers argue that receiving a no-match letter triggers a legal obligation to fire the employee. However, the no-match can be triggered by many causes, including an error in the data base. Despite the best efforts of the Bush Administration, at this writing courts have held that no-match letters do not create a legal obligation to discharge.

Advocates should file anti-retaliation charges under the statutes used by immigrant workers. In *Centeno-Bernuy v. Perry*, 302 F.Supp.2d 128 (W.D. N.Y. 2003), a federal court granted a preliminary injunction against retaliation by an employer that reported immigrant workers to various government agencies to deter them from exercising rights under the wage and hour laws.

Workers and their allies can also cite the ICE's own internal policy, Operating Instruction 287.3a, which discourages the agency from engaging in enforcement actions that interfere in a labor dispute.[33] In one campaign, a garment contractor called in the then-INS to raid its Manhattan factory as part of an effort to defeat the union. The raid led to removal proceedings against two workers. An Immigration Judge ruled that OI 287.3a was binding and therefore the workers could not be deported. However, do note that in a later case the Second Circuit held that the intervention of the immigration authorities at the request of a boss engaged in a union-busting campaign was not a defense to a workers' deportation. *Montero v. INS*, 124 F.3d 381 (2d Cir. 1997).

The labor movement in the United States has a long history of trying to keep workers from other nations out of this country. We believe that Planet Earth is a relatively small rock floating around in a large galaxy and even larger universe, and that dividing people based on where they happened to be born is not only absurd, but—like all divisions—will serve only to harm workers for the benefit of corporate profits. Borders are nothing but fictions which serve to obscure our common humanity as well as our class interests as working people.

CROSS-BORDER SOLIDARITY

Nothing that any of us do is more important than what has been called cross-border solidarity. It means reaching out to workers from other countries so as to create solidarity among an international working class. It puts flesh and blood on the idea that "My country is the world," expressed by Tom Paine, whose father was a corsetmaker; by William Lloyd Garrison, the son of a

---

33 Although common usage still refers to Operating Instruction 287.3a, the policy has been redesignated as 33.14(h) of the Special Agent Field Manual.

sailor; by Haymarket anarchist Albert Parsons, a printer who spoke these words to his judge and jury before being sentenced to death; and by railroad worker Eugene Debs, in a speech opposing World War I that led to a long federal prison term.

Here we discuss three ways of implementing cross-border solidarity, and the law (if any) relevant to each.

GOING THERE ONESELF

Except for travel to Cuba, the obstacle to travel to other countries is not so much the law but time and money.[34]

The rewards are enormous. More privileged organizers who have traveled abroad may not realize how rare an experience this is likely to be for lower-income workers. The movement in Youngstown made it possible over a period of a decade for about a dozen persons to attend a school run by the network of independent unions in Mexico, the Frente Auténtico de Trabajadores. One traveler had never been in an airplane before. For African Americans in particular, to spend time in a society where race and ethnic prejudice is dramatically less than in the United States (although by no means absent) was a heart-warming experience.

On another occasion the Workers' Solidarity Club of Youngstown sent people to Nicaragua to share, for a short time, in the daily life of ordinary workers. Ned Mann, a sheet metal worker, helped workers at Nicaragua's only steel mill to install a vent in the roof over an especially polluting furnace. Bob Schindler, an electric lineman, spent a week with a utility crew in Managua. He spoke no

---

34 If you want to go to Cuba, consult laborexchange@aol.com.

Spanish, they no English. Everybody got on fine, although Bob was appalled at the tools with which his Nicaraguan counterparts were obliged to do their dangerous jobs.

The next year Bob again used his annual vacation to go to Nicaragua, together with a younger fellow worker. They did what they could to finish the installation of the electric line in the far north of Nicaragua on which a young man named Ben Linder was working when he was killed by contra guerrillas.

DOING SOMETHING ABOUT SWEATSHOP LABOR

The most frequent form of solidarity with sweatshop workers in other countries has been the activity of students who pressured college administrations not to buy sports paraphernalia from companies that employ sweatshop labor abroad. When other tactics failed to bring results, students sat-in. Companies like Nike felt obliged to reveal the names and locations of subcontractors producing for the college market in the United States. The media reported gains at some of these overseas plants. While the students' committed action is to be lauded, it has been limited by a consumer-oriented approach and a dependency on third-party monitoring of factory conditions rather than worker self-organization. Far more effective and far less explored, is workers using their power as workers to exert power across borders.

CREATING CROSS-BORDER JOINT ACTIONS

The attitude of the labor movement in this country toward workers coming into the United States has often been defensive. Such hostility is prompted by an understandable fear that new participants in the work force, coming from countries in which wage levels are much lower, will undercut the wages and benefits won by unions in the United States.

Even the most progressive unions and rank-and-file movements have exhibited this attitude. In the late 1960s and early 1970s, for example, the United Farm Workers led by Cesar Chavez "used every means at its disposal to get undocumented migrants out of the fields. It reported workers to the Immigration and Naturalization Service and demanded that the agency arrest and deport them."[35]

Meantime, however, the number of undocumented immigrants in the United States rose from 3.3 million in 1980 to an estimated 11.5 to 12 million in 2007, and approximately one million new immigrants arrive each year.[24] Moreover, and never to be forgotten, it was these very same new immigrants and their families who poured into the streets on May 1, 2006, and reclaimed the historic workers' holiday of May Day for the entire working class of the United States.

Elsewhere we discuss how immigrant workers in the United States, whether or not undocumented, can use the law to organize. Here we simply suggest the idea that workers in the United States should begin to meet with their counterparts in the Global South to plan joint actions. Truck drivers, for example, instead of asking the United States Congress for ways to keep Mexican truckers out of the United States, should consider meeting with their Mexican counterparts to develop actions that would benefit all teamsters. And if General Motors workers in the United States contemplate a strike, why not approach Mexican workers for GM in Puebla, Mexico, and Canadian workers for GM in St. Catherine's, Ontario, and consider striking for goals that are continent-wide?

---

35 Jennifer Gordon, "Transnational Labor Citizenship," *Southern California Law Review*, v. 80, no. 3 (March 2007), p. 534.

Picture it: Baristas standing hand-in-hand with coffee farmers growing beans for Starbucks in Africa;[36] or retail workers at the Gap carrying out strategic actions in solidarity with workers making the clothes in Asia. Consider this globalization of worker solidarity the grassroots counter-offensive to the proliferation of corporate trade deals like NAFTA and CAFTA.

---

36 *Ibid.*, pp. 504, 535–36.

CHAPTER 6
CONCLUSION:
ANOTHER WORLD IS POSSIBLE

S tan Weir, who inspired the original version of this booklet, had a question that he used to ask students in his classes on labor education. The question was, "What's the funniest thing that ever happened where you work?"

It was a good question. When we laugh, we are usually feeling relaxed, confident, in control of our immediate situation. When workers laugh, it is often because they have had the kind of experience discussed above in the chapter on "Work to Rule." Perhaps a foreman has spectacularly screwed up. Perhaps a worker, and those near him or her on the line, have won one of those small victories that help a person to make it through the day.

In recent years students and others have repeatedly demonstrated in opposition to summit meetings of the capitalist nations, as in Seattle, Quebec City, and Genoa, Italy. In Seattle in 1999, the International Brotherhood of Teamsters and United Steelworkers of America assisted members to attend the demonstration because they wished to protect the livelihood of workers in the United States against imports and immigrant workers from abroad. Reportedly, the unions made an effort to keep their demonstrating members separate from the rowdier students, but many workers slipped under the arms of marshals to join the students in direct action downtown.

The motto of these student demonstrators against corporate "globalization" and "neo-liberalism" is, "Another world is possible!" The authors believe that another world is not only possible but inevitable, if we work hard enough for it. We encourage you to affirm it also.

What would "another world" at work be like? That is the most important question any reader should take away from this booklet. We challenge you to answer it.

Actually, perhaps we already know most of the answer. The universal testimony of workers in all settings is that things go better on the night shift when there are fewer white shirts (supervisors) to interfere with getting the job done right.

What if there were **never** any white shirts to interfere? What if workers and communities ran the business themselves?

People will say, "That's radicalism!" We've been called worse. Why shouldn't the democracy we demand in the political arena extend into the workplace where all of us spend so much of our lives? As a matter of fact, in situations with which we are familiar—Barcelona, Youngstown, Pittsburgh, Nicaragua, Argentina—workers showed that they could run the places when they worked without interference from above. The signs in Youngstown read, "If you don't want to make steel here, we will."

BIOGRAPHY

Staughton Lynd taught American history at Spelman College and Yale University. He was director of Freedom Schools in the 1964 Mississippi Freedom Summer. An early leader of the movement against the Vietnam war, he was blacklisted and unable to continue as an academic. He then became a lawyer, and in this capacity has assisted rank-and-file workers and prisoners for the past thirty years. He has written, edited, or co-edited with his wife Alice Lynd more than a dozen books.

Daniel Gross is an organizer with the Industrial Workers of the World and a co-founder of the first union in the United States at the Starbucks Coffee Co. Mr. Gross is also the founding director of Brandworkers International, a non-profit organization protecting and advancing the rights of retail and food employees across the supply chain. Mr. Gross serves on the steering committee of the National Lawyers Guild Labor & Employment Committee.

INDEX

C

M

N

O

P

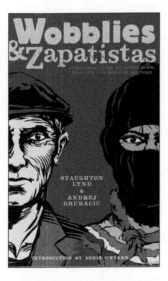

Wobblies and Zapatistas: Conversations on Anarchism, Marxism and Radical History
Staughton Lynd and Andrej Grubacic
ISBN: 978-1-60486-041-2
$20.00

Wobblies and Zapatistas offers the reader an encounter between two generations and two traditions. Andrej Grubacic is an anarchist from the Balkans. Staughton Lynd is a lifelong pacifist, influenced by Marxism. They meet in dialogue in an effort to bring together the anarchist and Marxist traditions, to discuss the writing of history by those who make it, and to remind us of the idea that "my country is the world." Encompassing a Left libertarian perspective and an emphatically activist standpoint, these conversations are meant to be read in the clubs and affinity groups of the new Movement.

The authors accompany us on a journey through modern revolutions, direct actions, anti-globalist counter summits, Freedom Schools, Zapatista cooperatives, Haymarket and Petrograd, Hanoi and Belgrade, 'intentional' communities, wildcat strikes, early Protestant communities, Native American democratic practices, the Workers' Solidarity Club of Youngstown, occupied factories, self-organized councils and soviets, the lives of forgotten revolutionaries, Quaker meetings, antiwar movements, and prison rebellions. Neglected and forgotten moments of interracial self-activity are brought to light. The book invites the attention of readers who believe that a better world, on the other side of capitalism and state bureaucracy, may indeed be possible.

"An exquisite contribution to the literature of human freedom, and coming not a moment too soon."
—David Graeber, author of
Fragments of an Anarchist Anthropology

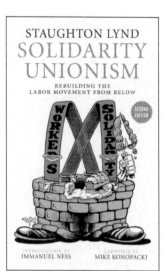

Solidarity Unionism:
Rebuilding the Labor
Movement from Below,
Second Edition
Staughton Lynd
Introduction by Immanuel Ness
Illustrated by Mike Konopacki
ISBN: 978-1-62963-096-0
$14.95

Solidarity Unionism is critical reading for all who care about the future of labor. Drawing deeply on Staughton Lynd's experiences as a labor lawyer and activist in Youngstown, OH, and on his profound understanding of the history of the Congress of Industrial Organizations (CIO), *Solidarity Unionism* helps us begin to put not only movement but also vision back into the labor movement.

While many lament the decline of traditional unions, Lynd takes succor in the blossoming of rank-and-file worker organizations throughout the world that are countering rapacious capitalists and those comfortable labor leaders that think they know more about work and struggle than their own members. If we apply a new measure of workers' power that is deeply rooted in gatherings of workers and communities, the bleak and static perspective about the sorry state of labor today becomes bright and dynamic.

To secure the gains of solidarity unions, Staughton has proposed parallel bodies of workers who share the principles of rank-and-file solidarity and can coordinate the activities of local workers' assemblies. Detailed and inspiring examples include experiments in workers' self-organization across industries in steel-producing Youngstown, as well as horizontal networks of solidarity formed in a variety of U.S. cities and successful direct actions overseas.

This is a tradition that workers understand but labor leaders reject. After so many failures, it is time to frankly recognize that the century-old system of recognition of a single union as exclusive collective bargaining agent was fatally flawed from the beginning and doesn't work for most workers. If we are to live with dignity, we must collectively resist. This book is not a prescription but reveals the lived experience of working people continuously taking risks for the common good.

*Solidarity Unionism
at Starbucks*
Staughton Lynd and Daniel Gross
Illustrations by Tom Keough
ISBN: 978-1-60486-420-5
$4.95

Legendary legal scholar Staughton Lynd
teams up with influential labor organizer
Daniel Gross in this exposition on solidarity
unionism, the do-it-yourself workplace
organizing system that is rapidly gaining
prominence around the country and around
the world. Lynd and Gross make the
audacious argument that workers themselves
on the shop floor, not outside union officials,
are the real hope for labor's future. Utilizing
the principles of solidarity unionism, any group of co-workers, like the workers
at Starbucks, can start building an organization to win an independent voice at
work without waiting for a traditional trade union to come and "organize" them.
Indeed, in a leaked recording of a conference call, the nation's most prominent
union-busting lobbyist coined a term, "the Starbucks problem," as a warning
to business executives about the risk of working people organizing themselves
and taking direct action to improve issues at work.

Combining history and theory with the groundbreaking practice of the model
used by Starbucks workers, Lynd and Gross make a compelling case for
solidarity unionism as an effective, resilient, and deeply democratic approach
to winning a voice on the job and in society.

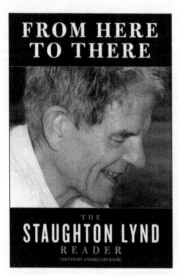

From Here to There:
The Staughton Lynd Reader
Staughton Lynd
Edited with an Introduction by Andrej Grubacic
ISBN: 9781604862157
$22.00

From Here To There collects unpublished talks and hard-to-find essays from legendary activist historian Staughton Lynd.

The first section of the *Reader* collects reminiscences and analyses of the 1960s. A second section offers a vision of how historians might immerse themselves in popular movements while maintaining their obligation to tell the truth. In the last section Lynd explores what nonviolence, resistance to empire as a way of life, and working class self-activity might mean in the 21st century. Together, they provide a sweeping overview of the life, and work—to date—of Staughton Lynd.

Both a definitive introduction and further exploration, it is bound to educate, enlighten, and inspire those new to his work and those who have been following it for decades. In a wide-ranging Introduction, anarchist scholar Andrej Grubacic considers how Lynd's persistent concerns relate to traditional anarchism.

"Staughton Lynd's work is essential reading for anyone dedicated to implementing social justice. The essays collected in this book provide unique wisdom and insights into United States history and possibilities for change, summed up in two tenets: Leading from below and Solidarity."
—Roxanne Dunbar-Ortiz

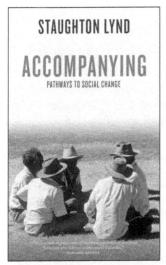

Accompanying:
Pathways to Social Change
Staughton Lynd
ISBN: 9781604866667
$14.95

In *Accompanying*, Staughton Lynd distinguishes two strategies of social change. The first, characteristic of the 1960s Movement in the United States, is "organizing." The second, articulated by Archbishop Oscar Romero of El Salvador, is "accompaniment." The critical difference is that in accompanying one another the promoter of social change and his or her oppressed colleague view themselves as two experts, each bringing indispensable experience to a shared project. Together, as equals, they seek to create what the Zapatistas call "another world."

Staughton Lynd applies the distinction between organizing and accompaniment to five social movements in which he has taken part: the labor and civil rights movements, the antiwar movement, prisoner insurgencies, and the movement sparked by Occupy Wall Street. His wife Alice Lynd, a partner in these efforts, contributes her experience as a draft counselor and advocate for prisoners in maximum-security confinement.

"Since our dreams for a more just world came crashing down around us in the late 1980s and early 1990s, those of us involved in social activism have spent much of the time since trying to assess what went wrong and what we might learn from our mistakes. In this highly readable book, Lynd explores the difference between organizing and accompanying. This book is a must-read for anyone who believes a better world is possible."
—Margaret Randall

Organize!
Building from the Local
for Global Justice
Edited by Aziz Choudry, Jill
Hanley & Eric Shragge
ISBN: 9781604864335
$24.95

What are the ways forward for organizing
for progressive social change in an era
of unprecedented economic, social, and
ecological crises? How do political activists
build power and critical analysis in their
daily work for change?

Grounded in struggles in Canada, the
United States, Aotearoa/New Zealand, as
well as transnational activist networks, *Organize!: Building from the Local for
Global Justice* links local organizing with global struggles to make a better
world. In over twenty chapters written by a diverse range of organizers,
activists, academics, lawyers, artists, and researchers, this book weaves a
rich and varied tapestry of dynamic strategies for struggle. From community-
based labor organizing strategies among immigrant workers to mobilizing
psychiatric survivors, from arts and activism for Palestine to organizing in
support of Indigenous Peoples, the authors reflect critically on the tensions,
problems, limits, and gains inherent in a diverse range of organizing contexts
and practices. The book also places these processes in historical perspective,
encouraging us to use history to shed light on contemporary injustices and how
they can be overcome. Written in accessible language, Organize! will appeal
to college and university students, activists, organizers and the wider public.

Contributors include: Aziz Choudry, Jill Hanley, Eric Shragge, Devlin Kuyek,
Kezia Speirs, Evelyn Calugay, Anne Petermann, Alex Law, Jared Will, Radha
D'Souza, Edward Ou Jin Lee, Norman Nawrocki, Rafeef Ziadah, Maria Bargh,
Dave Bleakney, Abdi Hagi Yusef, Mostafa Henaway, Emilie Breton, Sandra
Jeppesen, Anna Kruzynski, Rachel Sarrasin, Dolores Chew, David Reville,
Kathryn Church, Brian Aboud, Joey Calugay, Gada Mahrouse, Harsha Walia, Mary
Foster, Martha Stiegman, Robert Fisher, Yuseph Katiya, and Christopher Reid.

"To understand the world, you have to try to change it. That's
what the authors of this fine set of essays and meditations
have taken to heart. The result? Some of the best insights on
power, organizing, and revolution to be found."
—Raj Patel, author of *The Value of Nothing*

New Forms of Worker Organization:
The Syndicalist and Autonomist Restoration of Class Struggle Unionism
Edited by Immanuel Ness
Foreword by Staughton Lynd
ISBN: 978-1-60486-956-9
$24.95

Bureaucratic labor unions are under assault. Most unions have surrendered the achievements of the mid-twentieth century, when the working class was a militant force for change throughout the world. Now trade unions seem incapable of defending, let alone advancing, workers' interests.

As unions implode and weaken, workers are independently forming their own unions, drawing on the tradition of syndicalism and autonomism—a resurgence of self-directed action that augurs a new period of class struggle throughout the world. In Africa, Asia, the Americas, and Europe, workers are rejecting leaders and forming authentic class-struggle unions rooted in sabotage, direct action, and striking to achieve concrete gains.

This is the first book to compile workers' struggles on a global basis, examining the formation and expansion of radical unions in the Global South and Global North. The tangible evidence marshaled in this book serves as a handbook for understanding the formidable obstacles and concrete opportunities for workers challenging neoliberal capitalism, even as the unions of the old decline and disappear.

Contributors include Au Loong-Yu, Bai Ruixue, Shawn Hattingh, Piotr Bizyukov, Irina Olimpieva, Genese M. Sodikoff, Aviva Chomsky, Dario Bursztyn, Gabriel Kuhn, Erik Forman, Steven Manicastri, Arup Kumar Sen, Verity Burgmann, Ray Jureidini, Meredith Burgmann, and Jack Kirkpatrick.

"This exciting collection provides substantial evidence that collective action by workers themselves is indispensable to advancing a strong labor movement. The book's global scope demonstrates that workers in the U.S. and beyond can learn much from the tactics, strategies, and historical struggles in other countries."
—Kim Scipes, author of *AFL-CIO's Secret War against Developing Country Workers: Solidarity or Sabotage?*

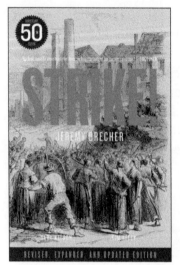

Strike!
50th Anniversary Edition
Jeremy Brecher
Preface by Sara Nelson
Foreword by Kim Kelly
ISBN: 9781629638003
$28.95

Jeremy Brecher's *Strike!* narrates the dramatic story of repeated, massive, and sometimes violent revolts by ordinary working people in America. Involving nationwide general strikes, the seizure of vast industrial establishments, nonviolent direct action on a massive scale, and armed battles with artillery and tanks, this exciting hidden history is told from the point of view of the rank-and-file workers who lived it. Encompassing the repeated repression of workers' rebellions by company-sponsored violence, local police, state militias, and the U.S. Army and National Guard, it reveals a dimension of American history rarely found in the usual high school or college history course.

Since its original publication in 1972, no book has done as much as *Strike!* to bring U.S. labor history to a wide audience. Now this fiftieth anniversary edition brings the story up to date with chapters covering the "mini-revolts of the 21st century," including Occupy Wall Street and the Fight for Fifteen. The new edition contains over a hundred pages of new materials and concludes by examining a wide range of current struggles, ranging from #BlackLivesMatter, to the great wave of teachers strikes "for the soul of public education," to the global "Student Strike for Climate," that may be harbingers of mass strikes to come.

"Jeremy Brecher's *Strike!* is a classic of American historical writing. This new edition, bringing his account up to the present, comes amid rampant inequality and growing popular resistance. No book could be more timely for those seeking the roots of our current condition."
—Eric Foner, Pulitzer Prize winner and DeWitt Clinton Professor of History at Columbia University

Friends of PM Press

These are indisputably momentous times—the financial system is melting down globally and the Empire is stumbling. Now more than ever there is a vital need for radical ideas.

In the many years since its foundingand on a mere shoestring—PM Press has risen to the formidable challenge of publishing and distributing knowledge and entertainment for the struggles ahead. With hundreds of releases to date, we have published an impressive and stimulating array of literature, art, music, politics, history, and culture. Using every available medium, we've succeeded in connecting those hungry for ideas and information to those putting them into practice.

Friends of PM allows you to directly help impact, amplify, and revitalize the discourse and actions of radical writers, filmmakers, and artists. It provides us with a stable foundation from which we can build upon our early successes and provides a much-needed subsidy for the materials that can't necessarily pay their own way. You can help make that happen—and receive every new title automatically delivered to your door once a month—by joining as a Friend of PM Press.

Here are your options (all include a 50% discount on all webstore purchases):
- $15 a month: Get 3 e-Books emailed to you
- $30 a month: Get all books and pamphlets
- $40 a month: Get all PM Press releases (including CDs and DVDs)
- $100 a month: Superstar—Everything plus PM merchandise and free downloads

For those who can't afford the shelf space, but can afford the solidarity and support, we're introducing *Sustainer Rates* at $100, $50, $20, $15, $10 and $5. Sustainers get a free PM Press T-shirt and a 50% discount on all purchases from our website.

Your Visa or Mastercard will be billed once a month, until you tell us to stop (you are not required to subscribe for any minimum amount of time). Or until our efforts succeed in bringing the revolution around. Or the financial meltdown of Capital makes plastic redundant. Whichever comes first.

Printed in the USA
CPSIA information can be obtained
at www.ICGtesting.com
JSHW082358140824
68134JS00020B/2154